Gender Diversity
in Government

Other Books in the Global Viewpoints Series

GLOBALVIEWPOINTS

Gender Diversity in Government

Avery Elizabeth Hurt, Book Editor

GREENHAVEN PUBLISHING

Published in 2020 by Greenhaven Publishing, LLC

353 3rd Avenue, Suite 255, New York, NY 10010

Copyright © 2020 by Greenhaven Publishing, LLC

First Edition

Articles in Greenhaven Publishing anthologies are often edited for length to meet page
requirements. In addition, original titles of these works are changed to clearly present
the main thesis and to explicitly indicate the author's opinion. Every effort is made to
ensure that Greenhaven Publishing accurately reflects the original intent of the authors.
Every effort has been made to trace the owners of the copyrighted material.

Cover image: HARALDUR GUDJONSSON/AFP/Getty Images
Map: frees/Shutterstock.com

Library of Congress Cataloging-in-Publication Data

Names: Hurt, Avery Elizabeth, editor.
Title: Gender diversity in government / Avery Elizabeth Hurt, book editor.
Description: First edition. | New York : Greenhaven Publishing, 2020. |
  Series: Global viewpoints | Includes bibliographical references and index.
  | Audience: Grade 9 to 12.
Identifiers: LCCN 2018057873| ISBN 9781534505575 (library bound) | ISBN
  9781534505582 (pbk.)
Subjects: LCSH: Women—Political activity—Juvenile literature. | Women
  politicians—Juvenile literature. | Women legislators—Juvenile
  literature. | Women heads of state—Juvenile literature. | Women political
  activists—Juvenile literature.
Classification: LCC HQ1236 .G461334 2020 | DDC 320.082—dc23
LC record available at https://lccn.loc.gov/2018057873

Manufactured in the United States of America

Website: http://greenhavenpublishing.com

Contents

Chapter 2: Causes and Effects of Gender Diversity

Chapter 3: Sexism and Gender Diversity in Government

Chapter 4: Looking Ahead

Foreword

> *"The problems of all of humanity can
> only be solved by all of humanity."*
> —Swiss author Friedrich Dürrenmatt

Global interdependence has become an undeniable reality. Mass media and technology have increased worldwide access to information and created a society of global citizens. Understanding and navigating this global community is a challenge, requiring a high degree of information literacy and a new level of learning sophistication.

Building on the success of its flagship series, Opposing Viewpoints, Greenhaven Publishing has created the Global Viewpoints series to examine a broad range of current, often controversial topics of worldwide importance from a variety of international perspectives. Providing students and other readers with the information they need to explore global connections and think critically about worldwide implications, each Global Viewpoints volume offers a panoramic view of a topic of widespread significance.

Drugs, famine, immigration—a broad, international treatment is essential to do justice to social, environmental, health, and political issues such as these. Junior high, high school, and early college students, as well as general readers, can all use Global Viewpoints anthologies to discern the complexities relating to each issue. Readers will be able to examine unique national perspectives while, at the same time, appreciating the interconnectedness that global priorities bring to all nations and cultures.

Material in each volume is selected from a diverse range of sources, including journals, magazines, newspapers, nonfiction books, speeches, government documents, pamphlets, organization newsletters, and position papers. Global Viewpoints is truly global, with material drawn primarily from international sources available in English and secondarily from US sources with extensive international coverage.

Features of each volume in the Global Viewpoints series include:

- An **annotated table of contents** that provides a brief summary of each essay in the volume, including the name of the country or area covered in the essay.

- An **introduction** specific to the volume topic.

- A world map to help readers locate the countries or areas covered in the essays.

- For each viewpoint, an **introduction** that contains notes about the author and source of the viewpoint explains why material from the specific country is being presented, summarizes the main points of the viewpoint, and offers three **guided reading questions** to aid in understanding and comprehension.

- **For further discussion** questions that promote critical thinking by asking the reader to compare and contrast aspects of the viewpoints or draw conclusions about perspectives and arguments.

- A worldwide list of **organizations to contact** for readers seeking additional information.

- A **periodical bibliography** for each chapter and a **bibliography of books** on the volume topic to aid in further research.

- A comprehensive **subject index** to offer access to people, places, events, and subjects cited in the text.

Global Viewpoints is designed for a broad spectrum of readers who want to learn more about current events, history, political science, government, international relations, economics, environmental science, world cultures, and sociology—students doing research for class assignments or debates, teachers and faculty seeking to supplement course materials, and others wanting to understand current issues better. By presenting how people in various countries perceive the root causes, current consequences, and proposed solutions to worldwide challenges, Global Viewpoints volumes offer readers opportunities to enhance their global awareness and their knowledge of cultures worldwide.

Introduction

> *"The silver lining is that women around the world are making substantial progress in reaching highest-level offices. That progress will continue and be sustainable as more women see that it is possible and desirable."*
>
> *—Laura Liswood, World Economic Forum*

In 2017, women held 23 percent of the parliamentary seats around the world. As of 2018, twenty women held the highest offices in their nations (heads of state or heads of governments) of 193 world governments. Some nations have more gender diverse governments than others, and you may be surprised by those that do.

Northern European nations do well when it comes to electing female and LGBTQ leaders. In a ranking of the world's nations according to percentage of women in parliaments, Sweden ranked seven, Finland was eleven, and Norway came in at thirteen. Farther south in Europe, France took the fourteenth spot, followed close by Spain at sixteen. The United Kingdom was farther down the list at thirty-eight, and Germany came in at forty-six.

On this side of the pond, the picture is mixed. Canada ranked 60, and the United States was way down the list at number 104. However, Cuba snagged the number two spot, Bolivia was ranked third, Mexico came in at number four, and Grenada was fifth. Two African nations rounded out the top six, with Namibia in the sixth place and Rwanda in the number one spot.

Things do seem to be improving. In November 2018, the American people sent a record number of women to the US Congress, making the 116th US Congress the largest class of female legislators in the history of the nation. Voters also sent record numbers of women to many state and local offices. (LGBTQ candidates did remarkably well in that election as well.) But despite the celebration, women still have a long way to go if they want to have a say in governing proportional to their numbers in the population.

At this point, women make up around 23 percent of the US House of Representatives, and roughly the same percentage of the US Senate. Their numbers in state legislatures vary, but across the nation women also fill just under a quarter of those seats. These numbers are historically encouraging. They are also abysmally low. Women make up roughly half the world's population. So why are they struggling to get a quarter of the seats in the world's governing bodies? Why are so many nations—often wealthier, more historically democratic nations—unable to elect representative bodies that are actually representative of their populations?

The writers of the viewpoints in *Global Viewpoints: Gender Diversity in Government* examine this question from a variety of perspectives and by looking at governments all over the world, from North America to East Asia. In the first chapter, viewpoints examine the current situation of women and LGBTQ candidates in nations from Africa to the West, and in majority Muslims countries. In chapter 2, writers take on the question of what causes the lack of gender diversity as well as ask what the world would be like if it had more women and LGBTQ leaders. The third chapter focuses on the role of sexism in keeping women out of leadership positions. Perhaps unsurprisingly, several of the viewpoints in this chapter deal with the question of why it seems so difficult for the United States to elect a female president. The last chapter takes a look ahead—particularly at how quotas might finally bring gender balance to the world's governments and what the results of that might be. There is much to find encouraging around the world, but as these viewpoints show, women and LGBTQ people have a lot of work to do before they are allowed to share equally the burden of serving their nations in elected office.

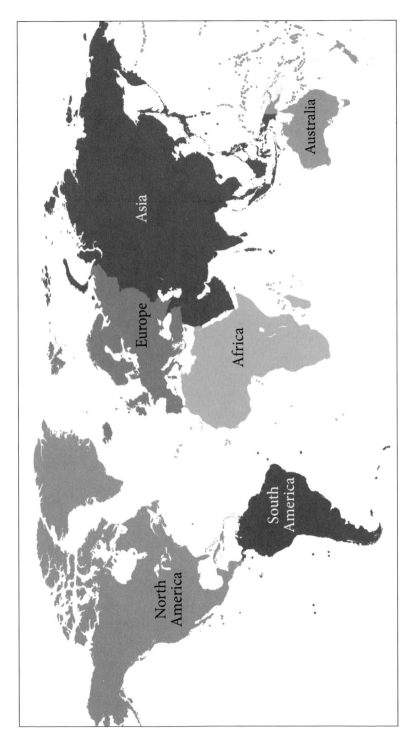

Gender Diversity in Governments Around the World

In Africa, Women Face Many Obstacles in the Battle for Equality

Gumisai Mutume

Over the past decade and a half, women in Africa have made a great deal of progress when it comes to gender parity in the continent's leadership. However, many women in Africa suffer disproportionately from poverty and still struggle for gender equality. In the following excerpted viewpoint, Gumisai Mutume explores the problems African women face and looks at possible solutions. Mutume is a Zimbabwean who writes for the New York–based United Nations publication Africa Renewal.

As you read, consider the following questions:

1. Why, according to the viewpoint, has this not translated to more equality throughout the continent?
2. What are some of the primary reasons mentioned that women in African countries are more likely to be poor than men there?
3. Why, according to the author, does the diversity of African nations make addressing problems of inequality more difficult there?

A decade ago, African women had reason to expect change following a much-heralded global conference that set ambitious targets to transform the lives of women across the

"African Women Battle for Equality," by Gumisai Mutume, United Nations Africa Renewal, July 2005. Reprinted by permission.

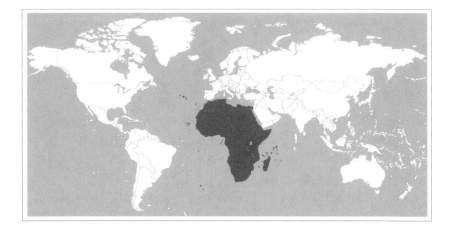

world. This year marks the 10th anniversary of that milestone event, the Fourth World Conference on Women, held in Beijing, China, in 1995. Like their counterparts elsewhere, African women are taking stock of progress and asking to what extent promised reforms have been implemented. They are also examining why progress has been limited in many countries and are seeking ways to overcome the obstacles.

During the last 30 years there have been a number of signs of improvement, UN Special Adviser on Gender Issues and Advancement of Women Rachel Mayanja told the 10-year review of the Beijing conference, in New York in March. There have been moves to implement the Convention on the Elimination of All Forms of Discrimination against Women (CEDAW), a UN protocol, as well as the development of new policies and guidelines and creation of networks of gender experts, she said, citing just a few examples.

However, over the same 30 years since the first World Conference on Women in Mexico City, "men have gone to the moon and back, yet women are still at the same place they were— that is, trying to sensitize the world to the unwarranted and unacceptable marginalization of women, which deprives them of their human rights," Ms. Mayanja told the delegates, who came from 165 countries.

In Africa specifically, women have made significant strides in the political arena over the past few years. The continental political body, the African Union (AU), took a major step by promoting gender parity in its top decision-making positions. In 2003 five women and five men were elected as AU commissioners. The following year, Ms. Gertrude Mongella was chosen to head the AU's Pan-African Parliament, where women make up 25 per cent of members. Another AU body, the African Peer Review Mechanism, which oversees standards for good governance, is led by Ms. Marie-Angélique Savané.

African women have also successfully promoted agreements that advance their rights. By the end of last year, 51 of the 53 AU member countries had ratified CEDAW, adopted in 1979 by the UN General Assembly and often described as the international bill of rights for women. And in 2003 activists succeeded in persuading their heads of state to adopt a protocol on the rights of women. They are now lobbying states to take the final step and ratify the protocol to make it enforceable.

[…]

Poverty Has a Woman's Face

For many African women, the Beijing platform and the various international instruments their governments have signed have yet to translate into positive changes in their daily lives. They remain at the bottom of the social hierarchy, with poor access to land, credit, health and education. While some of the agreements that African governments have ratified enshrine property and inheritance rights, in most countries women are denied those very rights.

Compounding the situation are setbacks such as the HIV/AIDS pandemic that is destroying the health of more women than men in Africa, eroding some of the development gains women had attained. As a result, poverty in Africa continues to wear a woman's face, notes Ms. Gladys Mutukwa of the Zimbabwe-based non-governmental organization Women in Law and Development in Africa (WILDAF). She finds it disturbing that 10 years after Beijing, African women are much poorer.

Between 1990 and 2000, the number of people living in poverty dropped in all developing regions except Africa, where it increased by more than 82 million. Women make up the majority of the poor, as much as 70 per cent in some countries. More often than not, men are more likely to find a job and enterprises run by men have easier access to support from institutions such as banks.

A UN Food and Agricultural Organization study on Benin, Burkina Faso, Congo, Mauritania, Morocco, Namibia, Sudan, Tanzania and Zimbabwe shows that women rarely own land. When they do, their holdings tend to be smaller and less fertile than those of men. Studies also show that if women farmers had the same access to inputs and training as males, overall yields could be raised by between 10 and 20 per cent.

Getting Girls into School

But perhaps the most inhibiting factor is that women in Africa continue to be denied an education, often the only ticket out of poverty. Disparities between girls and boys start in primary school and the differences widen up through the entire educational system. In total enrolment in primary education, Africa registered the highest relative increase among regions during the last decade. But given the low proportion of girls being enrolled, the continent is still far from the goal of attaining intake parity by the end of this year. By 2000, sub-Saharan Africa was the region with the most girls out of school, 23 million, up from 20 million a decade earlier.

The total number of children out of school has declined during the last decade. Between 1990 and 2000, worldwide enrolment in primary education increased from 596 million to 648 million, with the highest increase occurring in sub-Saharan Africa, which recorded a 38 per cent rise.

Policies specifically targeting girls were responsible for considerable improvements in countries such as Benin, Botswana, the Gambia, Guinea, Lesotho, Mauritania and Namibia. In Benin, for instance, the gender gap narrowed from 32 to 22 per cent, thanks to policies such as sensitizing parents through the media and reducing school fees for girls in public primary schools in rural areas.

The UN Educational, Scientific and Cultural Organization (UNESCO) reports that girls' enrolments rise relative to boys as the proportion of female teachers increases. Therefore an effective method of ensuring gender parity is to equalize the gender balance among teachers, a strategy Mauritania used to narrow the gender gap in primary schools from 13 to 4 per cent between 1990 and 2000.

Guinea employed a broader approach, making girls' education a national priority during the early 1990s. After assessing the challenges faced by girls in schools, the government embarked on programmes to build latrines, assist pregnant students, distribute free textbooks and increase the number of female teachers. By 2000, the country had more than doubled the number of girls in school and increased boys' attendance by 80 per cent. But in general, Africa has the lowest proportion of female teachers of any region.

Numerous other hurdles continue to hamper the expansion of education in Africa. Austerity programmes introduced in many countries during the 1980s constrained educational spending. Governments had little money to maintain existing schools or build new ones. At the family level, households that became poorer often faced the stark choice of deciding whom to send to school— and often it was the girl who stayed home. Costs of tuition, the requirement to wear uniforms, long distances between home and school, inadequate water and sanitation, all help to restrict girls' access to education.

By the time children go through high school and reach college, the gender gap has become even wider. "At the tertiary and university levels the low participation for women continues," declared African government ministers gathered in Addis Ababa in October to take stock of the continent's progress since Beijing. "Gender gaps are particularly pronounced in science, mathematics and computer sciences."

As with a range of other historically male-dominated subjects, an International Labour Organization (ILO) survey shows that women are starkly underrepresented in technical programmes in African colleges. The share of women enrolled in polytechnic courses ranges from 40 per cent in the Gambia to just 2 per cent in Zambia, the ILO reports. In Ghana, even though 30 per cent of all those attending polytechnics are women, only 1 per cent of the total taking technical courses are women.

Africa, however, has registered improvements in adult literacy rates, which rose 20 per cent between 1990 and 2000. The goal is to raise adult literacy rates by 50 per cent by 2015, from the 1990 level. About half of sub-Saharan African countries have registered moderate increases towards gender parity in this area, UNESCO reports. However, in some countries the female illiteracy rates are much higher than the regional average of about 50 per cent. In Burkina Faso it is 82 per cent, in Sierra Leone 79 per cent and in Benin and Ethiopia 77 per cent.

Channelling Money to Women

Many now acknowledge that to enable women to escape poverty, development policies should place more emphasis on their contributions to the economy. Even though women make up a significant proportion of the economically active population, their contribution is not fully recorded because they are mainly engaged in family farming or in the informal sector. In other cases, what they do, such as household work, is not considered an economic activity.

In agriculture, sub-Saharan Africa's most vital economic sector, women contribute 60–80 per cent of labour in food production, both for household consumption and for sale. But while they do most of the work, they lack access to markets and credit. In Uganda, women make up 53 per cent of the labour force, but only sell 11 per cent of the cash crops.

"I strongly hold the view that since days immemorial, women have played and continue to play a significant role in the economic and social development of their countries," says Namibia's Women's Affairs Minister Netumbo Nandi-Ndaitwah. "What is at stake is that they are not visible, not recognized and not rewarded for the hard work they do." She says that each country should allocate a percentage of its national budget to gender issues. "This request is based on the fact that to date no country allocates more than 1 per cent of its national budget to women and gender issues." Currently, resources for national programmes for the advancement of women come mainly from external partners.

Ms. Josephine Ouédraogo of the African Centre for Women in Addis Ababa says women's contributions through the household economy, which provides more than 70 per cent of food in Africa, are not adequately counted in national statistics. "Less than 10 African countries conduct systematic time-use or household surveys," she says. This makes it difficult to identify disparities between the sexes and design remedial policies.

To redress the bias in macroeconomic policies that favours men and boys at the expense of women and girls, a number of African countries have adopted a tool known as gender budgeting (see *Africa Recovery*, April 2002). Kenya, Rwanda, South Africa, Tanzania and Uganda are among the countries currently assessing their budgets along gender lines. This involves analyzing government spending choices and their impact on women and men, boys and girls, with the aim of better identifying disparities. That in turn can help mobilize more financing to narrow the gaps, for example by funding programmes to reduce the heavy time burdens on women or by improving their access to energy, water, transport and labour-saving technologies.

At a meeting in April 2004 to review women's progress since Beijing, non-governmental organizations (NGOs) from the

Southern African Development Community (SADC) called on its 14 member countries to adopt gender budgeting by December 2006.

Influencing Policy

Almost all SADC countries have a national government body that deals with gender issues. However, in the 10 years since Beijing, these units, departments or ministries "have become weak and unable to be responsive to the challenges presented by the struggle for gender justice," NGOs declared at an African Social Forum in Lusaka, Zambia. "Poor resource bases, few staff and no power or authority within governments to advance equality and justice for women are just a few of the constraints."

However, women in some countries in Southern Africa have moved into positions of political influence. In South Africa and Mozambique, for example, women hold 30 per cent of the seats in parliament. In February 2004, Mozambique became the first country in the region to appoint a woman as prime minister, Ms. Luisa Diogo. In Rwanda, women lead the world in representation in national parliaments. There, 49 per cent of parliamentarians are female, far more than the 30 per cent target specified in Beijing. The world average is just 15 per cent.

In 14 of 23 recent elections in African countries, women increased their parliamentary representation. Still, the situation is far from ideal. In the majority of these countries (20), women hold 10 per cent or less of parliamentary seats. In Madagascar, Mauritania and Niger, for example, they occupy less than 5 per cent of seats.

In some countries, the presence of women in parliament has made a difference in the adoption of gender-sensitive policies. Because of pressure from women, some countries now have affirmative action policies, such as quotas, to increase the number of women in decision-making positions. In South Africa, women parliamentarians succeeded in passing various pieces of legislation, such as those legalizing abortion, countering domestic violence and ensuring child support.

In Uganda, women parliamentarians helped to adopt legislation making rape a capital offence. In 2003, following a long delay, Mozambique passed a family law considered pivotal for the emancipation of women in that country. "If we had just one sex in parliament, the bill would have been weaker," says the country's higher education minister, Ms. Lidia Brito.

Because the continent is so diverse, the problems are very complex, says Ms. Wariaru Mbugua of the Office of the Special Adviser on Gender Issues at the UN. "Therefore, in global debates, they should not be made simplistic or be reduced to a single denominator." For example, girls not only need access to primary education, but must also be protected from violence and harmful practices.

While there is a need to continue with basic strategies to lift women out of poverty and to halt HIV/AIDS, Ms. Mbugua says, "it is also important to put in place second- and third-generation strategies." These include ensuring that global trade agreements and new information and communications technologies provide immediate benefits to women. Empowerment of women, she says, should not be confined to a narrow range of sectors within countrics, but should also "ensure the equal participation of women in fast-moving global processes."

"Equality Is Still Not a Reality"

From 28 February to 11 March 2005, as part of the 49th session of the UN Commission on the Status of Women, more than 80 government ministers, 1,800 other government delegates and 2,600 representatives of non-governmental organizations, from 165 countries, convened in New York for the 10-year Review and Appraisal of the Beijing Declaration and Platform for Action.

"Ten years after Beijing, this review called attention to the many areas where women's equality is still not a reality—continuing high rates of violence against women in all parts of the world, including in armed conflict, increasing incidence of HIV/AIDS among women, gender inequality in employment, lack of sexual and reproductive health rights and a lack of equal access under the law to land and property, to name a few," said Ms. Carolyn Hannan, director of the UN's Division for the Advancement of Women.

The meeting adopted a declaration calling for the "full and effective implementation of the Beijing Declaration and Platform for Action … essential to achieving the internationally agreed development goals, including those contained in the Millennium Declaration."

So far, four international conferences on women have been held—Mexico (1975), Copenhagen (1980), Nairobi (1985) and Beijing (1995).

Campaign to Ratify Women's Protocol

Gender activists are intensifying efforts to obtain the minimum 15 ratifications needed to bring into force a protocol to the African Charter on Human and People's Rights aimed at promoting gender equality. Once in effect, the Protocol on the Rights of Women would provide a legal framework for women's rights and require states to develop laws that prohibit discrimination.

The protocol states that every woman has the right "to the recognition and protection of her human and legal rights." It includes articles on equality in marriage, access to justice and political participation, protection of women in armed conflict and the provision of education, training and health care. It also upholds women's rights to housing and inheritance. The rights of widows and the special protection of elderly women and those with disabilities are also covered. The protocol contains guidelines on ending traditional practices such as female genital mutilation, which it condemns as harmful to the health of women and girls. Signatories will have to report periodically on progress and to provide financial resources to implement the rights enshrined in the protocol.

"For African populations and societies, the absence of a legal framework of reference to fight against violations of women's rights currently constitutes a real handicap for the optimal participation of women in the development of their countries and of Africa," writes Ms. Kafui Adjamagbo-Johnson of the non-governmental Women in Law and Development in Africa. She notes that economic and social rights that are constantly violated, either deliberately or out of ignorance, would be better protected under the protocol.

In Latin America, Activists Say Bringing More Women to the Open Government Movement Will Advance the Cause of All Women

Yamila García and Veronica Alvarez

The Open Government Partnership (OGP) is an organization that brings together reformers from a variety of nations in the effort to make governments more inclusive, responsive, and accountable to their citizens. In the following viewpoint, Yamila García and Veronica Alvarez argue that in Latin America, women are getting better access to jobs. However, they are largely absent from leadership in political parties, unions, and corporations. More women in the open government movement would, they argue, advance the interests of women in all areas. García and Alvarez are leaders in the OGP.

As you read, consider the following questions:

1. Why, according to the viewpoint, does the OGP seek input from women of all walks of life?
2. How do the authors explain that basic human rights are a necessary step in advancing equality?
3. What two key factors do the authors mention are necessary for strengthening the autonomy of women?

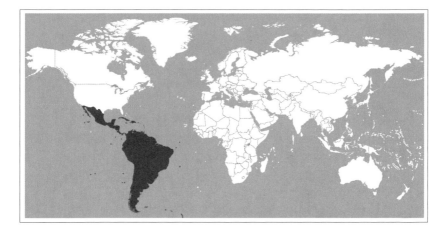

In late October 2015, during the Global Summit of the Open Government Partnership, we participated in the first meeting of women from different countries of the world that work on different themes of open government, with the goal of strengthening democracy in Latin America.

Our first meeting, held at the cultural hub Punto Gozadera in Mexico City, marked an important milestone. It gathered some 20 women from various countries, occupations and backgrounds, who are working on transparency, civic and technological innovation, civic hacking and open data. They are all seeking to increase civic participation and achieve the broader objective of making governments more transparent and accountable. This was an opportunity for dialogue and for sharing ideas and visions to strengthen the role of women in the open government realm.

We gathered many perspectives from women that work in civil society organizations and Latin American governments, as well as academics, hackers, journalists and activists. The dialogue led to a key common conclusion: we need to put together a task force of women leaders from all different sectors to set the stage for gender diversity in government policies, foster women's leadership in decision making and public policy, ensure gender mainstreaming in open government processes, favor the inclusion of diverse social groups and make our work more visible in order to ensure the participation of more women in open government initiatives.

Advancing gender equality and closing the inequality gap means working in pursuit of basic human rights and, given the current context, represent critical components of the global efforts around the Agenda 2030 for sustainable development. Strengthening and empowering women, through building more opportunities to participate in the public arena, means strengthening and empowering communities and states in the 21st century.

Moving Toward Open States

Today, governments are becoming aware of the need to incorporate mechanisms to change the culture and advance the open government framework. This is evidenced by the fact that, five years after its launch in 2011, 70 countries are now members of OGP. This large group of countries seeking to transition to more open governments holds key political potential to bring attention to gender equality as a tool to achieve more equal and human rights–centered democracies.

We are seeing growth in spaces for making governments more transparent, collaborative and participative in order to transform governments that have traditionally been opaque. We have also seen growth in the sharing of information, innovative experiences and perspectives, as well as the implementation of meaningful public policy. However, it is clear that these spaces are dominated by male leadership.

It is often said that the lack of female leadership in the open government movement is a result of a lack of skill or due to women's personal decisions; it has been claimed that women have not shown interest in this topic. However, this fails to account for the widespread gender inequality and the broader inequality that prevails in our societies.

To Achieve Equality for Women, We Must Close the Gender Gap in Local Governments

Recently, a new wave of women leaders is emerging at local level. Cities like Paris, Tokyo, Washington, Rome, Madrid, Sydney, Surabaya, Cape Town, Bucharest, Barcelona, or more recently Montreal, have elected female mayors in the past few years—most of them for the first time. Today, we have more females running for office and being elected as mayors that ever before. Yet, the proportion of women mayors is still a minority.

Although the global share of women elected to local government is currently unknown, with no official statistics of how many female mayors are currently in office, we can find some studies that have analyzed this issue. In 2015, UCLG [United Cities and Local Governments] estimated that fewer than five percent of the world's mayors were women and just 20 percent of local councilors worldwide were females. Additionally, the City Mayors Foundation, an international think tank dedicated to urban affairs, found out that, as of July 2017, only 26 cities of the 300 largest metropolises were governed by women, which is equivalent to around 8.6 percent. As a result, we could say that just around 5–10 percent of world's cities have women as mayors. Therefore, although the number is rising with recent elections, the proportion of women mayors is still very low.

Diversity of all forms in political representation is key to ensure equitable and inclusive cities and communities. Gender equality is one of them. Women's leadership and participation at every level of decision-making is crucial to achieve equality and inclusiveness. Therefore, closing the gender gap in political participation at local level and defining and implementing urban policies with a gender view should be a priority for cities around the world. Are our cities ready to lead gender-sensitive cities and promote gender equality at all levels?

"How Serious Is Gender Inequality at Local Government Leadership? A Quick Assessment of Women Leading Cities and Gender Equality," by Ana Isabel Duch and Pascual Berrone, IESE Business School, December 5, 2015.

Women, Inequality and Politics in Latin American Countries

The open government movement is not an isolated idea, and it is impacted by the same issues that surround the public, social and cultural domains in every country. Therefore, the lack of female leadership is not solely a manifestation of a condition of the open government movement, but a consequence of a broader societal context.

Two key factors that allow for strengthening autonomy of women and, therefore, their ability to make decisions, are education and employment. In the last decades, we have successfully advanced towards closing the education gap, including in higher education. However, this has not yet been successfully translated into equality in job opportunities: we have not yet broken the glass ceiling or achieved equal status and number in leadership roles.

Latin America is no exception. In this region, women are getting better access to jobs, including in the legislative branch (largely as a result of quotas) and academia. However, women are still mostly absent from political party leadership, union leadership, and corporate leadership. For example, only six women have been elected as president in the past 50 years in Latin America. This executive decision-making position has historically been dominated by men, and this is mirrored in ministries, subnational executive branches, and the majority of institutional structures. Women only reach certain heights. And when they do, they are generally subject to a higher level of scrutiny than their male counterparts.

This trend is also present in the open government movement, in open data and civic innovation, and tightly linked to technological innovation: women often occupy lower-status positions, but rarely hold decision-making roles, and therefore have low visibility. There is often an overlap with other types of inequality, including socio-economic.

It must be a priority for us to develop an inclusive and cross-cutting open government agenda where every voice is part of the creation and implementation of innovative and effective public policies for transparency, collaboration and participation. Open government initiatives that are designed to strengthen democracy will not reach their full potential as long as they fail to promote gender and racial equality.

OGP Women

Months after our meeting in the cultural hub in Mexico City, we gathered in the second meeting for women during the Regional Americas Meeting in Montevideo, Uruguay, last June. We made progress in the creation of a partnership of women leaders from civil society, academia, government, international bodies, and corporations to further the participation of women.

#MujeresOGP seeks to represent a channel for communication and impact for greater visibility of women working on open government, as well as a mechanism for creating knowledge for influencing decision makers that advance transparency, accountability, trust building and the creation of mechanisms for collaboration toward open states.

We now have to identify key women and motivate them to join the open government movement in their own countries. For that purpose, we will launch in the coming months a platform that includes mechanisms for dialogue and identification of activities that will strengthen bonds and actions to promote gender equality. Over the past month, we have been creating a women's directory with a growing number of participants, currently 130. Our ultimate goal is to build a community of women capable of channeling specific demands for public policies to further equality.

In Rwanda, Women Receive Mixed Messages About Leadership

Gregory Warner

Rwanda is often cited as the country with the most female representation in Parliament. In the following viewpoint, Gregory Warner takes a close look at the status of women in Rwanda and reports that despite their representation in government, Rwandan girls and women live in a world where feminism is seen as something for Americans—and not a good thing. Warner is a foreign correspondent and host of Rough Translation, *National Public Radio's international journalism podcast.*

As you read, consider the following questions:

1. According to this viewpoint, what is "being American" short for in Rwandan culture?
2. What is the historical reason for the large number of women in the Rwandan government?
3. What was the "Catch-22" faced by the women's debate team and described in this viewpoint?

I n high school, Mireille Umutoni aspired to be a club president rather than just secretary. And why not? She lives in a country where women seem to face no barriers, no discrimination.

In the parliament, for example, women hold more than half the seats. No country has a better record than that.

"It's the No. 1 Country for Women in Politics—but Not in Daily Life," by Gregory Warner, NPR, July 29, 2016. Reprinted by permission.

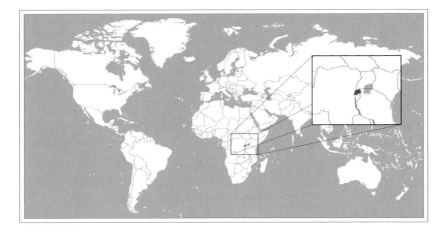

And in a ranking of countries by how they had narrowed the gender gap, Mireille's homeland came in sixth in the world. The US was No. 28.

There's just one problem: Mireille lives in Rwanda. And even though Rwanda is arguably the most pro-woman country in the world, feminism is not seen as a good thing. In fact, it's something of a dirty word.

In high school, Mireille found that teachers and students took for granted that the head of a club should be a boy. When she would stand up in front of her class and ask, "Why can't the head be a girl?" they would tell her, "That's for Americans. You're trying to be an American."

Being "American" was shorthand for being too aggressive, too liberated, too selfish. The message was clear: You're doing this for yourself, not for the good of your country. "They'd say, 'You don't belong in Rwanda,'" Mireille recalls. "'You don't even belong in Africa!'"

And when she did finally become head of a club—the debating club in her all-women's college—she faced another struggle: Could she and her team members succeed in the male-dominated world of collegiate debate?

When it comes to the roles of men and women, Rwanda is clearly a complicated place.

How the Genocide Changed Gender Roles

Following 100 days of slaughter in 1994, Rwandan society was left in chaos. The death toll was between 800,000 and 1 million. Many suspected perpetrators were arrested or fled the country. Records show that immediately following the genocide, Rwanda's population of 5.5 million to 6 million was 60 to 70 percent female. Most of these women had never been educated or raised with the expectations of a career. In pre-genocide Rwanda, it was almost unheard of for women to own land or take a job outside the home.

The genocide changed all that. The war led to Rwanda's "Rosie the Riveter" moment: It opened the workplace to Rwandan women just as World War II had opened it to American women.

In America, most WWII opportunities were short-lived. Millions of men came home after the war to claim their former jobs while women returned to domestic roles or jobs like nurse, teacher or secretary.

It wasn't until the 1960s that a new generation took up the call for equal opportunity.

In Rwanda, that's not what happened.

The call for equality was led not by thousands of women but by one man—President Paul Kagame, who has led the country since his army stopped the genocide. Kagame decided that Rwanda was so demolished, so broken, it simply could not rebuild with men's labor alone. So the country's new constitution, passed in 2003, decreed that 30 percent of parliamentary seats be reserved for women. The government also pledged that girls' education would be encouraged. That women would be appointed to leadership roles, like government ministers and police chiefs. Kagame vowed to not merely play catch-up to the West but leapfrog ahead of it.

The country embraced Kagame's policies and even went beyond his mandatory minimum. In the 2003 election, 48 percent of parliamentary seats went to women. In the next election—64 percent. Today Rwandan politics is cited as a model of gender inclusiveness.

This change from the top down was possible partly because of the nature of Rwanda's leadership. Kagame had a broad popular mandate for sweeping change—he had led Rwanda's army to stop the genocide. He's a strongman military ruler who allows little dissent or free speech. His word—and his vision—are often the country's command.

But even though the change was dramatic and swift, how deep was its impact? Can a country truly transform its core culture from the outside in?

If the example of the American women's movement is any indication, it was only after decades of women comparing experiences, envisioning what a different life might look like and then launching a movement, that change could occur. And never without struggle.

So what happens when a country skips the social upheaval and goes straight to the pro-women policies? When you take an aggressive shortcut through history, what do you leave behind?

When Empowerment Ends at the Front Door

Justine Uvuza wondered that, and decided to find out. A Rwandan herself who had grown up in a refugee camp in Uganda and then moved back to Rwanda in 1994, after the genocide, she worked for a while for the Kagame government promoting Rwanda's pro-women policies. She was curious how much progress had been made. So when she was getting her Ph.D. at Newcastle University, she returned to Rwanda to interview female politicians about their lives—not just their public positions but their private lives, with their husbands and children. She found with rare exception that no matter how powerful these women were in public, that power didn't extend into their own homes.

"One told me how her husband expected her to make sure that his shoes were polished, the water was put in the bathroom for him, his clothes were ironed," Justine says. And this husband wanted not only his shoes laid out in the morning, but his socks placed on top of the shoes. And he wanted it done by his wife, the parliamentarian.

Justine heard countless stories like this—women were still expected to perform even ceremonial domestic duties. It was rarely an option to outsource such tasks to a maid or get your husband to shoulder more work at home. Some women feared violence from their husbands if they didn't comply with these expectations, and one said that she had felt so trapped, she had contemplated suicide.

Justine says that for some of these women, the very real strides that they were making outside the home could feel less like liberation and more like a duty to be fulfilled. Being a "good Rwandan," as she termed it in her research, meant both being patriotic—serving her country through her public work and career—but also being docile and serving her husband. As a result, Justine said, a female politician could stand up in parliament, advocating for issues like stronger penalties for sexual violence and subsidized maxi-pads for the poor, but find herself scared to speak out about the oppression in her own home.

And so Justine would end each interview asking these female legislators what seemed to her to be an obvious question: Would they support a Rwandan women's movement? A movement to change not just the public roles for women but to re-evaluate gender relations on all levels? Would these powerful Rwandan women be willing to stand under the banner of feminism?

Almost all of the women said no. Feminism? "That's not Rwandan," they told her. "That's for Westerners."

Justine was not shocked. In fact, she had held the same views earlier in her life. She says that because of the way that gender equality came so rapidly to Rwanda, from the outside in, with no psychological buildup or women's lib movement, it was harder for these politicians to talk about equality without appearing disloyal, not just to their spouses but to their country.

She wishes a debate over the limits of equality could take place in Rwanda.

The Next Generation

And that's the debate that Mireille Umutoni Sekamana found herself part of. Born in 1995, she was frustrated by the anti-woman attitudes she faced in high school. When it came time to pick a university, she applied to the Akilah Institute for Women, Rwanda's first all-women's college, which was established in 2010 as a three-year vocational school. Akilah wasn't as prestigious as the four-year universities that some of her peers elected to attend. But Mireille wanted to be in a place where girls could lead clubs and ask a lot of questions in class without worrying about sounding too selfish, too American, too foreign.

When Akilah launched a debate team, Mireille volunteered as captain. It would be the first all-female college debate team in the country's history. In March 2015, barely two weeks after the debate team was formed, the female debaters of Akilah arrived at their first competition. They lasted 45 minutes, whomped in the very first round by one of the best schools in the country, the Kigali Institute of Science and Technology, or KIST. As Mireille's teammates saw it, they had lost for two reasons. One was that they hadn't yet mastered the debating rules. The second, more embarrassing reason was that they had acted like "girls"—specifically, the traditional stereotype of Rwandan women.

"They were 'acting like women' ... shy, quiet, and the voice does not go too high," says Martine Dushime, the one woman on the opposing KIST team. "[Rwandan women] have to be humble, speak slowly and all that. And that does not match with debate, seriously!"

If they were going to stay in the game, the Akilah team's women needed to find a way to be as confident onstage as they were in class. They had to change how they saw themselves—"to make sure that [they] feel powerful enough to take on anybody," said Samiah Millycent, an English teacher at Akilah and the debate team coach.

Power Posing

Samiah would later call it "the power game." One by one, before their weekly debating practice, each debater would walk to the front of the room, strike a "power pose," and say something to remind everyone in the room that she is powerful. That she is a winner. Week after week they repeated these phrases—"I'm a debater and I'm the winner today"—willing themselves to believe that it was true.

In a way, the girls were doing what their country had done: taking on a new pose, looking in the mirror and declaring themselves to be new, better and hopefully more successful.

Three months later, after weekly practices and doing mock debates, they returned for another countrywide competition, brimming with confidence.

The other contestants weren't buying it. They were literally pointing, laughing, saying "Really? They're back?" And Samiah says that even when the emcee was introducing the schools, saying, "Welcome to the debaters from this school … and the debaters from that school"—he introduced the Akilah team not as the debaters but "the ladies from Akilah."

"And he said it in a sarcastic way," Samiah said. "And we were like, 'God, why do people just have to look at us and feel like we don't deserve to be standing on the same podium with them?' So I told the girls, 'Girls, the task that we have today is to show these people that we didn't come to just grace the occasion, we came to take the trophy with us.'"

Each team was assigned an opponent. The Akilah team was pitted against KIST—the same team that trounced it in the previous competition. Next, the judges picked the topic the teams were to debate, out of eight possible topics announced the night before. The one topic that the Akilah team wanted, the topic the women knew they were going to rock, was, "This House Believes That Developing Countries Should Adopt Western Feminism."

So when the judges announced that the topic the team would debate was the very one they wanted, the Akilah team could barely contain its excitement.

For them, the phrase "Western feminism" symbolized all the ways they hoped to challenge gender relations and advocate for genuine equality.

That is, until the women went off to draw a piece of paper that would state which side of the debate they would have to argue. And they found out they had to argue … against.

To win this debate, the first-ever all-women's team had to make a persuasive case that Rwanda would not be better off if women were as free as men to choose how to live their lives.

In other words, to win, the team would need to argue for preserving many traditional gender roles—the opposite of what the women believed.

It was a real Catch-22.

A Daring Moment of Truth

The first team to take the stage was not Akilah but the KIST team, which argued for adopting Western feminism in Rwanda. Martine Dushime, the team's only woman, argued that Western feminism really means that women must get involved in their own movement: "Women standing their ground and saying, 'We want this,' not hiding behind the government policies."

The time was at hand for Akilah to figure out how to be winners. In the minutes before the teammates took their place onstage, they dug down deep into their own lives. They started to remember phrases they had heard over the years, phrases flung at women who stand up for themselves: "The man is always the head." "A marital spat is the woman's fault." An attention-seeking woman is "bad for her family."

The Akilah team boldly and confidently took the stage to spout phrases about why Rwandan women shouldn't be too bold or confident. "Copycats never learn" became the team's catchphrase, summing up all of Rwanda's anxiety about Western influence. "Why should we adopt something that is taking away our own originality?" Mireille said. The crowd roared.

And that's when, Mireille says, she had this moment onstage—looking out over the sea of mostly men's faces, knowing that there were government officials in the audience. She could tell that her team's argument was striking a chord. And she had this moment of thinking, "Uh oh."

Was it true that being a "good Rwandan" would always feel at odds with being an outspoken Rwandan woman? Would she herself always feel like an outsider—an interloper—in her own country?

The women won that debate. But they did not know: Had they won because they were superior debaters with newfound confidence? Or because they were so confidently arguing for the status quo? And did it matter?

"Ahh, it feels good when you actually convince the judge so the judge says you are the winners!" says debater Francoise Nyiratunga in our interview several months after the victory.

In the end, Francoise, Mireille and the rest of the team decided they didn't care how they won. Francoise says that, like any powerful debater, they got a confidence boost from arguing precisely what they did not believe: "Like to say a shoe is not a shoe, and you convince someone that a shoe is actually not a shoe!"

That confidence carried them to victory. They won the next round, and the next. That afternoon, they took home the trophy. And now, more than a year later, as the team has continued to compete, it has gained a substantial following of young women, some of whom have joined the debate club. Others have launched their own all-women's teams at other schools. "When we won," Mireille says, "it was a motivation to other girls."

The story of the Akilah team suggests that these young women found a way to be true to themselves as winners, not just good Rwandans.

But what about Rwanda? What about a whole country?

Can a nation at odds with its own values eventually change itself from the outside in?

The answer Justine gave me is that real change takes time. Taking a shortcut can get you somewhere fast, but it leaves the next generation to circle back and address changes that were left undone.

She told me that after all her interviews with the female politicians, she had to destroy the transcripts of those conversations. It was part of the rules of her university research. But it was more than that. For some of the women, this promise of anonymity was the only way she could get them to talk to her with candor.

Justine not only erased all the tapes; she took the typed transcripts and, page by page, set them on fire.

But she didn't follow the rules to a T. She kept a single copy of the interviews in a place that only she knows. She hopes that one day, these kind of stories will be heard by the people of Rwanda. Then, she says, the whole country will finally be ready to have that debate about how to move forward.

In Saudi Arabia, Pakistan, and Afghanistan, Women See Representation in Government and Violence at Home

Jessalyn Allen

In the following viewpoint, Jessalyn Allen argues that even though women in Muslim countries face a great deal of discrimination and violence, both at home and in public, they also have surprisingly high representation in their governments. Allen examines issues such as the difference between "standing for" and "acting in favor of" the people one represents, as well as the gap between political and cultural realities. Allen wrote this article for the World Citizens' Press, a platform for writers interested in international affairs.

As you read, consider the following questions:

1. How does violence toward women in Muslim countries compare to violence toward women in the West?

2. Allen mentions several theories that attempt to explain the contradiction between women's cultural and political roles. How do these contrast with each other?

3. Do you think quotas for women in government are a good idea? Why or why not?

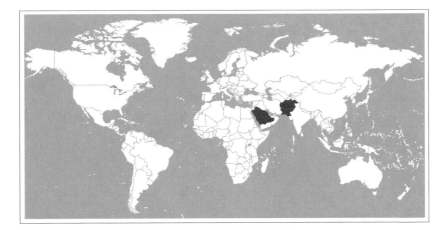

I n the western world, general perception of Muslim-majority countries is that women in these areas are violently subjugated. Of course, violence against women takes place across the globe: the World Health Organization reports that internationally, approximately 1 in 3 women (35%) experience sexual or physical violence. However, there is still merit to this claim. Saudi Arabia, where 99% of the population is Muslim and 99% of people feel Sharia law should be "the law of the land," is perceived as the worst country in the world in terms of gender equality. A 2006 study found that in Afghanistan, where approximately 99% of people are Muslim, 85% of women report having experienced "physical, sexual, or psychological violence or forced marriage." In Pakistan, an 87% Muslim country where 84% of people are in favor of making Sharia law "the law of the land," Amnesty International found that women "face discrimination and violence in the home and in public" and that thousands of cases of violence against women and girls are documented yearly, incidents including murder, rape, and domestic violence. It is widely speculated that thousands more cases go unreported.

Despite the oppression women face in these and other Muslim-majority countries, these women also have significant representation in their governments. Eight out of 49 (roughly 16% of) Muslim-majority states have had a female head of state. In

Saudi Arabia, 19.9% of parliament seats are women. In Pakistan, not only is 20.6% of their parliament women, but they appointed female Prime Minister Benazir Bhutto from 1988 to 1990 and 1993 to 1996, for a total of 5 years in office. In Afghanistan, a whole 27.7% of their legislative body is women, even exceeding the international average of 23.4%. In comparison, only 19.9% of legislative seats in the United States are filled by women, and the US has never had a female president.

Indeed, although women in many Muslim countries experience violence, these same countries also significantly represent women in their governments. This reality is rather baffling, considering that these two facts seem to be mutually incompatible. With particular attention to Saudi Arabia, Afghanistan, and Pakistan, how can the relatively strong presence of women in the governments of these Muslim-majority nations be explained, considering that they also maintain high levels of violence against women?

Scholars have posited a number of explanations for this phenomenon, their answers encompassing all three principal theoretical paradigms. For instance, Amélie Le Renard offers a purely realist perspective in her assessment that the segregation of men and women's spaces in Saudi Arabia does not presuppose the division of a "male public sphere (for production) and a female private sphere (for reproduction)." She asserts that women have their own exclusively female spaces in government office, and that it is "the spread of the Saudi state's authority" and "the oil boom" that have caused a decline of "women's work" and the appearance that they are marginalized. Her focus on the relative power of the Saudi government as an explanation for how women can both face segregation and be a force in that government is plainly realist, as realists are concerned with balances of power in the international system. Though her claim is valuable in its recognition of governments' power and statewide economic success as factors affecting women's representation, its exclusion of culture is a weakness.

At the opposite end of the paradigmatic spectrum, constructivists tend to be hyper-focused on the role of culture in perplexing circumstances such as these, even to a fault. Isobel Coleman dabbles in feminist theory in her constructivist writing that "Islamic feminists insist that Islam … is progressive for women," and that through "arguing for women's rights within an Islamic discourse," they can "expand opportunities for women, even within culturally and religiously conservative Muslim countries."

Mansoor Moaddel questions the existence of any connection between "gender hierarchy and religiosity" in Saudi Arabia, and indicates that religiosity has no positive effect on the promotion of gender hierarchies in the political sphere. Indeed, Valentine Moghadam presents an alternative constructivist theory, as he rejects the "ubiquity of Islam in politics and culture." Moghadam focuses on "dynamics of patriarchy and the contradictions of development and social change" in Afghanistan and Pakistan as an explanation for how political actualities—like female presence in government—may not coincide with broader social realities. These constructivist theories, while critical in their consideration of internal ideological contributors, are lacking in their appreciation of domestic non-cultural elements and foreign influences.

Sarah Bush, as well as Lynne Manganaro and Nicholas Alozie, offer liberal perspectives in their explanations of this conundrum. Bush attributes significant numbers of women in government to the presence of quotas for female representatives in many Muslim-majority nations, as do Manganaro and Alozie. However, Bush describes that quotas are adopted "directly, through post-conflict peace operations" as well as "indirectly, by encouraging countries … that depend on foreign aid, to signal their commitment to democracy by adopting quotas." Manganaro and Alozie suggest, similarly, that while quotas may be descriptively effective in affording representation to Afghani women, "they have been engineered externally and characteristically tied to foreign development assistance, often amidst stiff internal resistance."

Both liberal accounts link women's representation to quotas set as a result of their countries' foreign policy relationships, though like realist approaches, they seem to neglect ideological factors.

Although these various theories are all defensible, there seems to be an under-acknowledged middle ground between the liberal and constructivist perspectives. Liberal explanations are the most adept in describing the realities of women in Saudi Arabia, Afghanistan, and Pakistan, as all three implement quotas prescribing women a certain number of seats in their parliamentary bodies. The important realization here is that while quotas may offer a sense of true representation, widespread violence against women can continue behind this guise of democracy as a cultural and religious norm.

As mentioned, women hold 19.9% (30) of 150 seats in Saudi Arabia's unicameral Majlis al-Shura: Consultative Council. In early 2013, Saudi King Abdullah appointed women to 30 council seats (20%): the first time in the country's history that women held political office. In 2015, women voted for the first time in municipal elections, yet they won only 20, around 1%, of seats. This speaks to the reality that women's considerable amount of representation is only propped up by the quota system, and that women still have little to no political agency otherwise.

Considering when King Abdullah took office, his actions were likely influenced by international institutions and foreign powers. For instance, his installment in 2005 was concurrent with bombings carried out by militant Islamic terrorist group al-Qaeda, though his regime openly arrested al-Qaeda members. In the same year, Saudi Arabia became a part of the World Trade Organization, after which the Saudi government engaged in a number of lucrative arms deals with Great Britain and the United States.

In 2013, after Abdullah appointed 30 women to the Shura council, he turned down a non-permanent seat on the UN Security Council because of international backlash over Saudi Arabia's backing of Syrian rebels. International institutions seemingly influenced Abdullah's policy, according to how much he stood to gain from them. Thus, it is imaginable that his creation of a quota for women's representation was for the benefit of positive international perception of his country and lucrative trade deals.

Although there are no government-issued statistics available on violence against women in Saudi Arabia, many scholars and individual case studies report that women face high (and increasing) levels of violence, particularly domestic. For instance, a woman is likely to suffer "several forms of abuse for refusing to comply with her husband's demands," such as physical, emotional, sexual, and economic-social abuses. In 2011, Amnesty International reported that women battle "discrimination in law and in practice and [are] subjected to domestic and other violence," and more specifically that "the law does not give women equal status with men" and "[subordinates] women to men in relation to marriage, divorce, child custody and freedom of movement." In fact, women were only just granted the right to drive by the Saudi King on September 27 of this year, by royal decree.

Women do indeed have significant representation in the Saudi Shura council, yet they also face extraordinary violence. In acknowledging that women's representation is only so inflated because of a quota system implemented to present a facade of democracy to foreign powers, it is possible to reconcile such representation with the amount of violence against women. Despite de jure representation, the vast majority of Saudi Arabian women have almost no agency and remain abused and oppressed.

Here, it is also worth considering the distinction between descriptive and substantive representation in government: "the variance between a representative 'standing for' or 'acting for' the represented population." Political theorist Hanna Pitkin delineates descriptive representation as the extent to which a representative resembles those they are representing, whereas substantive representation is "acting in the interest of the represented, in a manner responsive to them." Importantly, all members of the Shura council are appointed by royal decree of the monarch. Thus, it is likely they do not provide Saudi women descriptive representation, as the king would select women he feels will not challenge his agenda. Even more noteworthy is that while members of the Shura council can draft legislation to be presented to the king, he may dismiss or veto any such effort. In this way, Saudi women are not substantively represented either, as their presence on the council does not permit them to effectively act for the women they represent.

In Afghanistan, women hold 27.7% of seats in the Afghani bicameral National Assembly, which consists of the Meshrano Jirga, House of Elders, and the Wolesi Jirga, House of People. Women first earned the right to vote in Afghan elections in 1919, one year before US women gained suffrage, though this right was revoked and reinstated several times before most recently being implemented in 2004 with the creation of a new constitution. A committee was charged with drafting this constitution according to the Bonn Agreement following the overthrow of the Taliban in 2001 by allied forces including the United States and Great Britain. The Bonn Agreement was directly overseen by the UN and laid the foundation for US and NATO-backed state-building efforts. According to Article 83 of the 2004 Constitution, at least 68 of the Wolesi Jirga seats are reserved for women, roughly 26% (Fleschenberg, 2015). Also, in 2014, women turned out en masse to vote despite threats from the Islamic fundamentalist group, the Taliban, whose influence lingers.

It is notable that the quota to ensure traditionally-marginalized women's representation was only implemented after foreign (primarily western) states oversaw the establishment of a new government in 2001. Without foreign intervention, such a progressive, liberal constitution would probably not have been created, as fundamental Islamic groups would likely have remained in control.

Despite women's representation in government thanks to quotas, violence against and oppression of women still occurs frequently. 37% of Afghans feel honor killings of women who engage in premarital sexual activity are "often justified." A further 60% believe women should not be able to decide for themselves whether or not to wear a veil, while 65% think sons should have a greater right to parents' inheritance. 66% of Afghans "completely agree" that a wife must always obey her husband.

As in Saudi Arabia, despite being somewhat well-represented in their governments, Afghan women experience much discrimination. In both countries, women's representation is guaranteed thanks to quotas implemented according to other foreign (primarily western) states' influence, allowing widespread mistreatment of women to occur on other levels beneath the political facade.

Like Saudi Arabian women, Afghan women are not afforded substantive representation, though they are descriptively represented on some level. Since commencement of women's suffrage in 2004, women have voted in increasing number each election, affecting the outcomes of presidential and legislative elections. Nevertheless, women in the legislative bodies have been unable to act on behalf of the women they represent. President Harmid Karzai (the first elected president of Afghanistan), in office from 2004–2014, even toyed with women's rights as he used women to "woo the Taliban into peace talks." Incumbent president Ashraf Ghani's government (2014–present) has neither moved in favor or against women thus far. Accordingly, though Afghan women are descriptively represented, they are yet unable to affect their government's policy changes.

The history of Pakistan's quota for women in government is dissimilar to Afghanistan and Saudi Arabia's. Pakistan has experienced comparatively less western influence on its political affairs, and has progressed according to a slow-rolling grassroots women's rights movement for decades. In 1956, long before either Saudi Arabia or Afghanistan moved towards such things, Pakistan's government approved a constitution that ensured suffrage and reserved seats for women in the bicameral Majlis-e-Shoora (parliament) which consists of the Senate and National Assembly. Women are guaranteed 60 of 342 seats, about 18%. At present, women are represented even above and beyond the quota, at 20.6% representation.

What is more, Pakistan was the first Muslim country to appoint a female prime minister, as Benazir Bhutto was elected for a total of nearly 5 years in office. Though her incumbency was broken up by military coups, her election reveals that Pakistan's inclusion of women in government is not manufactured for the benefit of foreign powers or institutions, but instead is an organic movement that has developed over time.

Of course, Pakistani women still face a great deal of marginalization and violence. 31% of Pakistanis think honor killings are "often justified" and 64% believe a wife must always obey her husband. Women are subject to beatings, murder threats, rape, gang rape, acid burning, and even being set on fire, while women of lower classes experience so much domestic abuse that they perceive it "as part of their culture and tend to accept it as their fate." Dr. Tazeen Saeed Ali reports that "every second woman" in Pakistan suffers some form of domestic violence.

The political reality of women's representation in Pakistan is an organic, legitimate development, and the quotas in place to help ensure women's presence in government are a result of domestic policy changes over the course of decades. Regardless, there remains a disconnect between that political reality and what a large percentage of the population practices socially. In this way, women are both represented and experience violence in their everyday lives.

Unlike Saudi Arabia and Afghanistan, women in Pakistan are both descriptively and substantively represented. Civil society in Pakistan has gradually moved away from cultural and religious barriers to women's participation in government, resulting in a gradual, steady increase in their representation that is only partially propped up by their quota system. Women freely exercise their right to vote, and women in government descriptively stand for Pakistani women. Further, women legislators have moved many private bills concerned with women's rights issues, including domestic violence, allowance for women to inherit property, and prosecution of men accused of sexual harassment. Their actions have secured substantive representation for Pakistani women.

In all three countries in consideration—Saudi Arabia, Afghanistan, and Pakistan—quota systems allocate a certain number of legislative seats for women, affording them substantial representation in their governments. Nevertheless, while these quotas appear helpful in practice and offer the sense of true representation, women may continue to experience violence as a de facto cultural standard. As Dina Mansour cites in her article, the intersection of "culture and politics" subjects women to selective application of rights dictated by norms, culture and tradition, rather than law. In Saudi Arabia and Afghanistan, quotas have been implemented only in recent years as a result of exchanges with international institutions and other states. Saudi Arabian women enjoy neither descriptive nor substantive representation in their government, while Afghan women are represented only descriptively. In Pakistan, the current quota is the end product of many decades of grassroots women's rights movements and political turmoil, and women experience both descriptive and substantive representation. In any event, the disconnect between political reality and social reality explains how women in these Muslim-majority countries can be substantially represented in their governments and also systematically oppressed.

Subsequently, it is critical to move towards ensuring women representatives both accurately stand for and effectively act in favor of those they represent in all of these states and elsewhere. Such descriptive and substantive representation can be achieved through the promotion of open party politics, promotion of women's advocacy NGOs and women's rights groups, encouragement of women's participation in politics (particularly in rural areas), establishment of proportional representation, enforcement of laws curbing violence against women, and so on. A step towards eliminating the disassociation between the political and socio-cultural realities would be a simultaneous step towards eliminating all violence against women across the globe.

Throughout the West, the Future of Work Requires Diversity and Inclusion

David Cruickshank

In the following viewpoint, David Cruickshank argues that creating a diverse and inclusive work environment will lead to more women in leadership roles, both in business and in government. Here, the author focuses primarily on Europe, where he lives, and the United States. Cruickshank is chair of Deloitte Touche Tohmatsu Limited, a member of the World Economic Forum Chairman's Group, and a board member of the Social Progress Imperative.

As you read, consider the following questions:

1. What does the author see as a silver lining in the grim diversity statistics he reports?
2. What initiatives other than quotas does Cruickshank mention that help get more women in leadership positions?
3. How, according to this viewpoint, might millennials change the future of work and leadership?

The pace of technological change and the potential impact on the future of work is far greater than we've ever seen.

"The Future of Work Requires Diversity and Inclusion," by David Cruickshank, Deloitte Global, July 17, 2017. Reprinted by permission.

Organisations are faced with increasingly complex questions as technological capabilities continue to accelerate—they are now under pressure to completely rethink what work means, how employees are selected and trained, and how the workplace is designed.

As organisations navigate these technological and societal shifts, corporate boards will have a critical role to play. Diversity of thought—and of people—will be more vital than ever to ensure that boards are considering different perspectives and exploring challenges from every angle.

Yet despite repeated studies linking company performance to diversity and continued efforts to improve gender diversity on boards across the world, only 15 percent of all board seats and 4% of CEO and board chair positions are filled by women globally. This is according to Deloitte's recent *Women in the Boardroom: A Global Perspective* report. These findings underscore that board diversity continues to progress at an unacceptably slow pace.

But the study also reveals a potential silver lining. Gender diversity seems to have a multiplying effect: some diversity leads to more diversity. Organisations with women in the top leadership positions have almost double the number of board seats held by women. The inverse is true as well, with gender diverse boards more likely to appoint a female CEO or board chair.

With the percentage of women in leadership positions remaining so low around the world, the question remains: how can organisations promote greater gender diversity, particularly in their leadership ranks?

What We Can Learn from Gender Diversity Efforts Around the World

Gender quotas continue to play an important role in many countries. For example, since 2005 Norwegian legislation has focused on gender diversity on the boards of public limited companies—the first country in the world to do so. 42 percent of board seats are

Top Ten in Gender Equality

What's the first thing that comes to mind when you think of Iceland? Volcanoes? Geysers? Well, actually, it should be gender equality.

For nine years this tiny Nordic nation has held the top spot in the World Economic Forum's Global Gender Gap Index, which ranks 144 countries based on how close they are to achieving gender equality.

The *Global Gender Gap Report 2017* reveals that Iceland has now closed more than 87% of its overall gender gap.

But globally the gap has widened this year—for the first time since the annual report began in 2006. The average remaining distance to gender parity is now 32%, up from 31.7% last year. The report measures the equality between men and women in four key areas: health, education, economics and politics.

It's not all bad news. Many countries have bucked this depressing global trend and improved in the last 12 months, with more than half reducing their gaps.

The Top Ten:

1. Iceland
2. Norway
3. Finland
4. Rwanda
5. Sweden
6. Nicaragua
7. Slovenia
8. Ireland
9. New Zealand
10. Philippines

"These Are the World's Most Gender-Equal Countries," by Joe Myers, World Economic Forum, November 2, 2017.

held by women in Norway, a 7 percent increase from 2015.[1] Many other countries have, or are planning, to follow suit.

In the absence of gender quotas, some other countries have made progress through a combination of government, private sector, and investor initiatives. In New Zealand, while there are no legislated gender quotas, the government has committed to increasing women's participation on state sector boards and committees. These efforts seem to be paying off, 27.5 percent of board seats are held by women, an 11 percent increase from 2015.[1]

In the UK, where I live, initiatives sponsored by business and government have helped to increase boardroom gender diversity in FTSE 100 companies and a goal has been set to reach 33 percent women directors serving on FTSE 350 boards by 2020. Additionally, the 30% Club, a group of board chairs and organisations, of which I am a member, supports a voluntary approach to increasing gender diversity across UK companies. The group believes better gender balance can be achieved by setting measurable goals with a defined time table, supportive public policy, change driven by those in power, collaboration and a consistent series of actions and programmes, from schoolrooms to boardrooms.

In the US, there are no gender quotas, but some state governments have passed nonbinding measures in recent years to help increase women's representation on boards. Progress toward achieving true gender balance has been sluggish. In the future, collaborative efforts among investors and other stakeholders are expected to help move the needle as gender diversity is a topic investors are increasingly vocal about.

While the efforts to improve gender diversity around the world vary significantly from country to country, it is clear that intentional leadership in both the public and private sector is critical to achieving greater gender diversity in the C-suite and boardroom. Setting the right tone at the top is fundamental. This includes leadership from men because nothing will change without chair, board and CEO support, both of which tend to be dominated by men.

To Reach and Sustain a Diverse Workforce, Inclusive Cultures Are Critical

Diversity of course goes beyond gender. Race, sexual orientation, age, class, religion, ability, and many other factors must also be considered. The talent pool has never been more diverse and organisations are faced with unique challenges in attracting and retaining talent.

Building an inclusive culture is critical to sustaining a diverse workforce. People perform best when they feel valued, empowered, and respected by their peers. If organizations merely bring in diverse people and do not proactively attempt to include them, then those people are likely to feel disempowered and leave.

Millennials, who will comprise nearly 75 percent of the workforce by 2025, are a major force behind this thinking. For them, inclusion is not just about representation, but rather a collaborative environment that values open participation from individuals with different ideas and perspectives. They value inclusion as a critical tool that enables business competitiveness and growth and many consider a company's inclusion policies before accepting a job.[2]

Creating an inclusive and diverse work environment is not only the right thing to do, it is vital for businesses to survive in this era of rapid technological and societal change. The combination of diversity and inclusion delivers better business outcomes in terms of ability to innovate, responsiveness to changing client needs and team collaboration. And you can recruit and retain the best people.

Notes

1. Deloitte, *Women in the Boardroom: A Global Perspective*, 2017.
2. Deloitte, *The Radical Transformation of Diversity and Inclusion: The Millennial Influence*, 2015.

In Europe and the United States, LGBT Candidates Are Winning Elections

Annalisa Merelli

Women aren't the only people to strive for gender equality in the world's governments. This viewpoint takes a look at progress made by LGBT leaders. Currently, the number of openly LGBT world leaders is growing rapidly. In the following viewpoint, Annalisa Merelli gives a brief history of LGBT leaders and an overview of LGBT leaders currently serving their cities and nations. She also points out that the political positions and concerns of modern LGBT leaders go beyond gender issues. Merelli is a geopolitics reporter at Quartz.

As you read, consider the following questions:

1. In this viewpoint, the author discusses LGBT leaders at the local as well as the national level. After reading the previous viewpoints, can you explain why this is important?
2. Merelli points out that even though transgender issues had recently been at the fore in Virginia, Danica Roem won her race more on the issue of transportation than on gender issues. Why does the author think this important?
3. How might removing the party and left/right constraints from LGBT candidates help rather than hinder their election prospects?

"The LGBT Political Glass Ceiling Is Cracking Wide Open," by Annalisa Merelli, Quartz, June 20, 2018. Reprinted by permission.

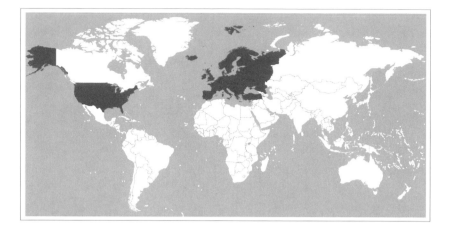

The list of countries that have been led by an openly LGBT person is short, but growing fast.

It was only in 2009 that Iceland's Jóhanna Sigurðardóttir was elected, becoming the first openly LGBT person in the world to serve as a prime minister. In 2011, Belgium's Elio Di Rupo became prime minister. In 2013, in neighboring Luxembourg, Xavier Bettle was voted prime minister—a position he still holds. He has since been joined by two additional LGBT leaders: Serbia's Ana Brnabić, and Leo Varadkar of Ireland, a country that only decriminalized same-sex relations in 1993.

These leaders belong to a club of openly LGBT politicians that was all but inexistent only 40 years ago, but is now finally reaching their nation's highest offices, while advocating for issues that go far beyond sexuality and gender identity.

It's the Moment(um)

With the exception of the Soviet Union's Georgy Chicherin, an openly gay Menshevik named commissar for foreign affairs in 1918, the first LGBT person to hold a prominent public office was Coos Huijsen—who came out as gay the year before he joined the Dutch parliament in 1977.

Today, at city, regional and national levels, several thousand openly LGBT politicians have entered the scene—a trend that shows no signs of slowing down. The 2017 elections in the US, for instance, saw important successes for LGBT candidates around America—primarily, but not exclusively, within progressive voters. The number of American LGBT mayors is up to 23—one of them, Peter Buttigieg, is a rising democratic star serving in conservative South Bend, Indiana who came out on the pages of his local paper while in office. Last weekend he married his partner as his town celebrated Pride with the rest of America. In the same year, in the UK, 35 LGBT representatives were voted into parliament (on both sides of the aisle).

As the US approaches the politically hot summer of 2018, a record number of LGBT candidates (over 400) are running for office—from city councils members to governor. They include high-profile personalities—such as infamous whistleblower Chelsea Manning, who will be contesting a Maryland Senate seat, and actor Cynthia Nixon, who is challenging New York's governor Andrew Cuomo. Perhaps most excitingly, this year's Texas governor's race features a major first: Lupe Valdez, who—if elected—would be the nation's only Latina and lesbian governor.

Coupled with the progress in terms of marriage equality and civil unions across the western world (as well as parts of Latin and South Africa), the LGBT political class ceiling—the so-called "lavender ceiling"—appears to finally be cracking. But how deep are these cracks? And what are their consequences?

Painting the Town Hall Rainbow

In a city like New York, home to many historic LGBT milestones, 36-year-old Corey Johnson is still making history. The New York City council speaker is not the city's first high-ranking LGBT politician; his predecessor, Christine Quinn, is gay, as are five of 51 current council members. But in addition to his sexuality and his youth, Johnson is the only HIV-positive elected official in New York state.

Despite the relative diversity of New York City's political scene, Johnson rejects the idea that being an LGBT representative shouldn't matter. "Being gay is not like having blue eyes," he says. He considers his sexual orientation an integral part of his identity—the way he lives, who he loves—and says it will always be associated with his political persona.

That persona is, after all, what got him here. Despite being co-captain of his Massachusetts high school's football team, Johnson says he was "an openly gay, despondent, suicidal teenager." LGBT leaders who came before him were his lifeline and role models—folks Harvey Milk and Larry Kramer, of whom he has photos in his office. Johnson hopes to serve the same role for the next generation. He is expected to run for mayor of New York City in 2021 (potential slogan: "Stop F---ing With Us"); were he to win, Johnson would be the first openly LGBT mayor in the city's history.

Johnson points out that voters across the political spectrum tend to choose candidates based on "bread-and-butter issues"—health care, education, welfare—more often than gender or sexual orientation. Danica Roem, for example, was elected last year as the first transgender member of the Virginia senate. While her sexual identity was part of the debate, Johnson says the race was ultimately "won on the issue of transportation."

Still, he cautions against a false sense of complacency. "One of the first things I said [after marriage equality was passed] was that people would pull back on their activism," Johnson says. Indeed, according to a survey published by GLAAD, a media-monitoring organization focused on LGBT rights, there was a shift in public support for LGBT cause in 2017. Today, more people are showing some amount of discomfort with LGBT issues and a growing number of non-LGBT people are becoming "remote supporters" rather than allies.

Unsuspected Places

Strong LGBT representation in New York City may be unsurprising. But elections in other parts of the world show acceptance spreading to new levels. Heavily Catholic Ireland, for instance, voted not only in favor of gay marriage, but in favor of an openly gay

Taoiseach (prime minister) in Leo Varadkar. Patriarchal, male-dominated, traditionally homophobic Serbia, too, surprised the world by electing a lesbian, Ana Brnabić, to lead the government. And while a map of the Middle East remains discouraging for LGBT rights, tangible progress is being made in Israel—even amongst conservatives.

Amir Ohana, who in 2015 became the first openly gay conservative representative in the Knesset (Israel's parliament), says LGBT acceptance in the country is growing, though it's "a matter of evolution, rather than revolution." Visibility is key to that evolution. "You can legislate against hate crimes, but you can't legislate against hate," Ohana says. The only way to fight hate is to encourage diversity.

The change in perception, he says, has been particularly impressive among ultra-orthodox Jews, which comprise an important component of Israel's population and political class. Barely a decade ago, Ohana recalls, members of ultra-orthodox political parties would speak about LGBT people as something that needed to be "treated, like the bird flu." The demographic has since become more tolerant, which he views as a consequence of increased familiarity with LGBT people like himself.

Ohana quotes a right-wing ultra-orthodox politician who said during a debate that he couldn't sanction same-sex marriage, but could acknowledged that LGBT people are part of society. "He would still vote against us," Ohana says, "but the terminology has changed." Simply by their mere existence and work in the Knesset, he says, members of the LGBT caucus managed to "get the homophobes into the closet."

Beyond Identity

In addition to representation, it's also important that LGBT candidates aren't reduced to just LGBT issues. This is a stance Ohana clearly embraces, as a member of the hawkish, right-wing Likud party. Back when he first joined Likud, many members "thought I was the first gay [person] they had ever met," he says.

Yet for them, as well as the larger Israeli society, "when they see me, 'gay' isn't the first thing that comes to mind, but my actions and views."

Ohana concedes that LGBT issues are typically the domain of progressives, but says that baking them into the conservative agenda taps into an electorate that would otherwise vote left almost by default. He likes to quote David Cameron, who "once said 'I do not support gay marriage despite being conservative but because I am conservative.'"

The current movement, however, seems to suggest something larger: LGBT issues finally transcending political affiliation, and becoming everyone's to care for, in turn freeing LGBT politicians to stand for whatever they please.

Periodical and Internet Sources Bibliography

The following articles have been selected to supplement the diverse views presented in this chapter.

Benjamin G. Bishin and Feryal M. Cherif, "The Big Gains for Women's Rights in the Middle East, Explained," *Washington Post*, July 23, 2018. https://www.washingtonpost.com/news/monkey -cage/wp/2018/07/23/womens-rights-are-advancing-in-the -middle-east-this-explains-why/?utm_term=.103e100cf95c.

Economist, "Ten Years On from Norway's Quota for Women on Corporate Boards," February 17, 2018. https://www.economist .com/business/2018/02/17/ten-years-on-from-norways-quota -for-women-on-corporate-boards.

Josie Glausiusz, "Would the World Be More Peaceful If There Were More Women Leaders?," Quartz, October 30, 2017. https:// qz.com/1115269/would-the-world-be-more-peaceful-if-there -were-more-women-leaders.

Devon Haynie, "Much of the World Has Had a Woman Leader. Why Not the U.S.?," *U.S. News & World Report*, November 4, 2016. https://www.usnews.com/news/best-countries /articles/2016-11-04/why-europe-asia-and-latin-america -elect-more-female-leaders.

Sarah Kliff, "The Research Is Clear: Electing More Women Changes How Government Works," Vox, March 8, 2017. https://www .vox.com/2016/7/27/12266378/electing-women-congress -hillary-clinton.

Catherine Rottenberg, "We Need Social Justice, Not Just More Women in Congress," Al Jazeera, October 3, 2018. https:// www.aljazeera.com/indepth/opinion/women-congress -change-181002143846035.html.

Didi Kirsten Tatlow, "As China Prepares for New Top Leaders, Women Are Still Shut Out," *New York Times*, July 16, 2017. https://www.nytimes.com/2017/07/16/world/asia/china -women-communist-party.html.

GLOBALVIEWPOINTS

Causes and Effects of Gender Diversity

The Most Common Excuses for Not Having Enough Women Leaders Are Myths

Kim Azzarelli and Deanna Bass

In the following viewpoint, Kim Azzarelli and Deanna Bass challenge common assumptions that keep women from reaching parity in politics, as well as in business and entertainment. They contend that the reasons cited for women's failure to have the same level of success as men are described as something wrong with women, rather than something wrong with the culture—something they call the "fix the women mentality." Here, the authors refute such myths one by one. Azzarelli is cofounder of the Cornell Center for Women, Justice, Economy, & Technology. Bass is the director of global diversity and inclusion at Procter & Gamble.

As you read, consider the following questions:

1. What myths hold back women, according to the authors?
2. According to the authors, women hold 40 percent of MBAs, 47 percent of law degrees, and 52 percent of professional jobs. Why then are women not making it to the top jobs in business and government?
3. Why are men needed to help women succeed, according to the viewpoint?

From the Golden Globes to this week's World Economic Forum in Davos, the topic on every group of leaders' agenda is "women." Thanks to movements like #MeToo and #TimesUp, and given the prospect of a record number of women running for office, women's voices are being heard like never before.

But if we want what's been dubbed "The Year of the Woman" to be more than a slogan, we also need significant numbers of women heading our biggest companies and institutions, the organizations that can drive real change. And that won't happen unless we recognize that the world still operates under a set of assumptions—we prefer to call them myths—that hold women back from reaching anything near parity in the upper ranks.

These myths go something like this: If only women would be more assertive. If only they would raise their hands and take more risks. If we could just fix the women, then the leadership roles that have so long eluded women would be theirs.

Do more. Be more. Change. While throughout history women were constrained by stereotypes that portrayed them as physically and emotionally frail, today's women bump up against the assumption that women's behavior is the reason they're stuck at about 17% to 20% of leadership positions worldwide.

This "fix-the-women" mentality places the onus for change on women, rather than on the real culprit: systemic flaws inherited from a time when the workplace was designed from a single perspective (male). As the latest sex-harassment scandals remind us, in the past, when women obeyed the norms of this workplace, they got nowhere. If they were "good sports" and brushed off misconduct as "boys will be boys," they were harassed all the more. And if they spoke up—well, no one listened. Or worse, they were fired.

Creating a workplace where women can lead requires that we stop trying to fix women, and debunk all the myths that feed into this mentality:

#1: The Women-Lack-Ambition Myth

To start, companies need to re-think their traditional notions of "leadership" and "ambition." Male behavior is not the be-all standard. Delivering on goals is.

From what we've seen, there is no female "confidence gap" or "ambition gap" among professional women. What we do know is that in women, confidence and ambition show up differently than they do in men.

For instance, studies show that men tend to overestimate their abilities in everything from math to entrepreneurship, while women underestimate theirs. Unfortunately, when a woman says she isn't qualified for a role, or a man says he is, we believe both—and use this as proof that women have a "confidence gap."

No negative label is put on men's behavior. Yet, what some call male confidence can also be seen as recklessness, that a potentially unprepared person is applying for an important job or running a business.

Misperceptions about women's behavior may account for their more difficult path up the corporate ladder. One report shows that women lobby for promotions at comparable rates to men, but are less likely to be promoted. Another study revealed that women ask for raises as often as men do, but get them less often.

#2: The Pipeline Myth: There Aren't Enough Qualified Women

In addition to rethinking "leadership," companies need to be intentional and creative in their hiring, both by promoting from within and recruiting outside the box.

As of mid-2017, 6% of companies in the Fortune 500, or 32 of them, had women CEOs. If we want to reach gender equality, we'd have to go from 6% to 50%.

We hear it frequently: There aren't enough women prepared to hold the biggest jobs—or who even want them.

But look again. To attain equality among Fortune 500 CEOs, companies would need to recruit just 218 women—and they're out there. The same thing goes for boards of directors. A board is usually 12 or 14 people. If your board is already 25% female, you need to add just three more women. Any company can find that.

The pipeline, in fact, is full of qualified women. Women hold almost 52% of all professional-level jobs in the US. They constitute 40% of MBAs from top schools and 47% of all law degrees. And yes, they want the big jobs. A Bain study showed that nearly half of new women employees aspired to the C-suite.

#3: The Man Myth: Advancing Women Hurts Men

When the new myths about women get busted, both women and men—and the companies they work for—benefit. One study shows that women-led startups may have a higher rate of return than the average male-run company. Another report says that companies with female CEOs perform three times better than S&P 500 companies headed predominantly by men.

It's also important to recognize, in this post-Harvey era, that men are the greatest allies women can have. Time and again we've seen men do the right thing: Stand up for women, fire miscreants—and in some instances put women into the leadership roles vacated by men. Most men want women to succeed.

Men can help by amplifying the voices of women in their companies—recognizing women's contributions and making sure they get credit. They can also make a difference by seeing gender stereotypes for what they are and alerting others to them, too.

A workplace where women are fully represented at every rung will be better for all. And that's no myth.

Religious Messages Can Influence Support of Gender Equality in Nations Around the World

Baha'i International Community

In the following viewpoint, the Baha'i International Community focuses on a series of meetings held at its offices in advance of the 2014 meeting of the UN Commission on the Status of Women. The participants quoted explore how religious messages impact views about gender and can give rise to patriarchal societies. While quotes from religious texts are often used to support suppression of women, this piece also points out that there is much in traditional religious texts that supports gender equality. The Baha'i International Community represents the worldwide Baha'i community, whose members come from every national, ethnic, religious, cultural, and socioeconomic background, representing a cross section of humanity.

As you read, consider the following questions:

1. What, according to this viewpoint, is the goal of this series of conversations?
2. What example do the authors provide as an illustration of gender equality in a religious text?
3. One person quoted here says that older generations convey the idea of sexist roles. Do you think this suggests that gender equality will be easier as today's youth take on more leadership?

"Impact of Religious Messages on Gender Equality Explored in Advance of Beijing + 20," Baha'i International Community. Reprinted by permission.

How can religious beliefs that place men above women be reconciled with international norms on gender equality? Can negative religious justifications about gender inequality be reversed? What is the impact of such messages across the lifespan of a human being?

These are among the questions being explored in a series of conversations about the connection between religious belief and gender equality over the next few months in advance of the March meeting of the UN Commission on the Status of Women (CSW), which is commemorating this year the 20th anniversary of the Fourth World Conference on Women and is known as Beijing +20.

The first such conversation was held 17 December 2014 at the offices of the Baha'i International Community (BIC). It focused on the impact of religious messages about gender during childhood.

"Interpretations of religious doctrines as assigning inferior status to women and girls have given rise to patriarchal systems which continue to obstruct women's full participation in society," said Bani Dugal, the principal representative of the BIC to the United Nations, in introductory remarks.

"Such messages of inequality are conveyed even before the birth of a child and continue on into old age," she said.

The aim of the series, which is being co-sponsored by the BIC, the United Nations Population Fund (UNFPA), UN Women, and the World YWCA, is to explore the impact of religious messages on gender equality along all of the major phases of life.

"It is our hope that we will through these conversations be able to become more conscious of the way we communicate and find ways to identify and convey positive messages that would be empowering to both girls and boys," said Ms. Dugal.

In January, she said, a meeting will be held to explore the impact of religious messages during adulthood, while the meeting in February will examine how older persons are affected by religious messages about gender.

In March, during the CSW itself—which this year will commemorate 20 years since the ground-breaking 1995 Fourth

Making Progress, but Still Running Behind

As nations around the world celebrate International Women's Day, the number of countries that have had a female leader continues to expand. But the list is still relatively short, and even when women have made it to power, they've rarely led for a long time.

Fifty-six of the 146 nations (38%) studied by the World Economic Forum in 2014 and 2016 have had a female head of government or state for at least one year in the past half-century. In 31 of these countries, women have led for five years or less; in 10 nations, they have led for only a year. The Marshall Islands, which is not included on the WEF list of countries, has also had a female leader for one year.

At least 13 additional countries have had women leaders who held office for less than a year, according to a separate analysis by Pew Research Center. Of these countries, Ecuador and Madagascar had women leaders for a total of just two days. In South Africa, a woman was president for a 14-hour stretch, but she had briefly served as acting president before; in all three countries, women leaders were replaced by men.

There are 15 female world leaders currently in office, eight of whom are their country's first woman in power, according to our analysis of data from WEF and other sources. While the number of current female leaders—excluding monarchs and figurehead leaders—has more than doubled since 2000, these women still represent fewer than 10% of 193 UN member states.

The list of women currently in office includes nine heads of state and eight heads of government. (Some leaders are both, and President of the Swiss Confederation Doris Leuthard is neither on her own—Switzerland's Federal Council collectively heads both state and government and leadership rotates between its seven members.)

The US and its neighbors have had little or no time under female leadership. The US and Mexico have never had a woman as chief executive, and Canada's first and only female prime minister served for just four months.

"Number of Women Leaders Around the World Has Grown, but They're Still a Small Group," by Abigail Geiger and Lauren Kent, Pew Research Center, March 8, 2017.

World Conference on Women in Beijing—there will be an event highlighting the entire series, she said.

The December conversation featured remarks by three panelists, followed by a lively exchange among all participants.

The panelists were Janet Karim, first secretary for social affairs of the Mission of Malawi to the UN; Maha Marouan, associate professor of African-American Studies and Women Studies at Penn State University; and Saskia Schellekens, special adviser to the UN Secretary General's Envoy on Youth. Three youth respondents— Selamawit Adugna Bekeleo from Ethiopia, Mtisunge Kachingwe from Malawi, and Christian Guaman from the United States— also participated.

Ms. Karim discussed some of the tensions she observed in Malawi when some religious groups sought to block new national laws promoting equality of women and men.

"Quotes from religious books such as the Bible were often quoted as proof that women were not meant to be leaders," said Ms. Karim.

She observed, however, that there is much in the sacred writings of many religions to support equality. "When Jesus rose from the dead, the first people he met were women," she said. "So that should show that God is fair."

Dr. Marouan said religion plays a very important role in most people's lives, whether directly or indirectly. "Religion can be a source of health, it can create community and support," she said.

"Religious discourse can also contribute to gender inequality, sometimes in direct ways and sometimes in subtle ways," she said.

Explicit messages could be as simple as "women don't deserve to have education," she said. "Or it could be as implicit as telling girls that women cannot be leaders."

Ms. Schellekens said "cultural and religious practices based on patriarchal norms and women's repression are major obstacles that can reinforce stigma and discrimination and can also affect the design and implementation of laws and policies."

While religious belief "can be a source of sustenance" for many, she said, "religious expectations can be barriers to the empowerment of women and girls in particular."

"Expectations can be especially harmful to girls," she said. "They may find that they are restricted, especially as they come of age, in their freedom of movement, in their educational development, and in their economic opportunities."

Boys, on the other hand, may feel a sense of entitlement—and they may feel pressure to "take on behaviors that are a risk to others and also themselves," she said.

All of these factors, she said, "translate into the development challenges and realities that we are faced with today."

"We must continue to act within the guidelines of the Beijing declaration and other initiatives that push for ending gender discrimination and inequality—and religious leaders and communities have to play their part in being part of this, and it's our role to engage with them," she said.

"We must also remind ourselves that human rights violations may never be justified in the name of culture or religion or tradition."

In her response, Ms. Adugna Bekeleo, who was raised as an Orthodox Christian in Ethiopia, discussed the importance of religion at the grassroots—and the necessity of differentiating between genuine religious teaching and "cultural" practices that have been added on, such as early marriage or female genital mutilation (FGM).

"For people who have never been to school, [religion] is where you get your knowledge," she said. "Every social gathering is based on religious concepts or has the presence of at least one religious leader."

She said many of these leaders now seek to prevent things like early marriage or FGM, in part because of work done by her NGO that works with them to discuss whether such practices are supported by theology.

"It's always about interpretation," she said.

Mr. Gauman of the United States talked about how he has come to understand some messages in the media subtly reinforce the idea that men are superior.

"Most men in today's society are given a more powerful role," he said, something he indicated was wrong and the fault of previous generations.

"Older generations have conveyed this thought of sexist roles until now," he said.

After the panelists made initial remarks, participants engaged in a wide ranging conversation that included the sharing of personal experiences with a religious message and gender equality.

In the United States, Double Standards and a Unique Political System Stand in the Way of Gender Parity in Leadership

Laura Liswood

Most observers were stunned when Hillary Clinton was narrowly defeated by Donald Trump in the 2016 US presidential election. In the following viewpoint, Laura Liswood explores some of the reasons it might not have been so surprising. The author begins by explaining why the US political system makes it difficult to elect women to the presidency. She then explores how the Trump campaign and the media exploited stereotypes about women during Clinton's campaign. Liswood is secretary general of the Council of Women World Leaders.

As you read, consider the following questions:

1. Why, according to the author, is the United States falling down the list of countries with female political empowerment?
2. Why does the US system of government make it more difficult to elect a woman president?
3. How, according to the viewpoint, did the media treat Clinton and Trump differently in the 2016 US presidential campaign?

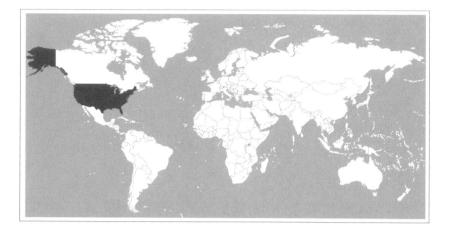

I t was supposed to be the day America would catch up with history and the rest of the world. Finally, the US would elect its first woman president.

It turns out that the catch-up will be delayed. When it comes to political empowerment, the United States is ranked 73rd out of 143 countries, according to the World Economic Forum's Global Gender Gap Report 2016.

The US is slowly falling down the list—not because its record on electing women is getting worse, but because other countries are getting substantially better. Today there are 60 members of the Council of Women World Leaders, all of them current or former freely elected heads of state or government as president, prime minister or chancellor. On the list of countries that have had such a leader in the past 50 years, the US is dead last.

The obvious question is, why? Why can't the world's most powerful nation elect a women president?

In trying to parse how much of this failure is the unpredictability of politics' rough-and-tumble process and how much is sexism, I separate the causes into two categories: the seed and the soil. The seed is the individual candidate. The soil is the ground in which that candidate has to try to prosper: the institutional structures and processes that either facilitate change or throw up barriers.

Winner Takes All

The United States and its winner-take-all system is tough soil for new growth to take root in. The electoral college, not the popular vote, determines who gets elected, giving more weight to outliers in middling states like Michigan or Ohio. In this system, third-party candidates can act as spoilers, preventing major party candidates from gaining a clear advantage in some states.

The hurdle for women is lower in countries in a parliamentary system, where the multiple parties can agree to back one another's leaders in coalitions. Parliamentary elections also put more parties in play. The more parties in play, the more opposition leaders there are. And since women often become opposition leader before they become prime minister, there are more opportunities for women to take the top job. Women also often find an entry point to the presidency in countries where the prime minister is the executive and the president wields more symbolic "soft power."

More than 100 countries, furthermore, promote women's chances to lead with some sort of quota system, requiring a certain minimum number of seats in parliament to be filled by women. Women are given the chance to hone their political skills as a member of parliament or deputy, establishing a well-stocked pipeline of experienced women legislators prepared to run for the high office.

In the US, where no such quotas exist, the percentage of the House and Senate seats held by women seems to plateau at about 20%, never attaining what many regard as a critical mass of 35%. Affirmative mechanisms are highly unpopular and unlikely to be enacted.

Quotas don't advance unqualified women but remove in-group favouritism and closed social networks, so qualified women can advance.

Question of Stamina

Fighting to lodge in this forbidding soil, the seed has its own disadvantages. Women simply do not fit the archetype of a leader in a country that stakes its superpower status on its military might. Men are presumed to be strong until they show otherwise. Women must prove they have strength, which is what made Donald Trump's attack on Hillary Clinton's "stamina" so effective. Using this code word, he played on Americans' unconscious fear that Clinton was not strong enough to be commander-in-chief.

Nearly all of the female leaders in the Council of Women World Leaders have experienced scrutiny of their hair, dress, voice and style that men get much more rarely. In the seemingly endless US election campaign, the objectification of Hillary Clinton went beyond hyper-scrutiny to misogynistic name-calling, with anti-Clinton T-shirts and signs reading "Trump the bitch."

Trump was accused of this kind of misogyny, and his rise gave voice to an unsettling loss of centrality among some supporters, encouraging them to abandon political correctness, as they saw it, and vocalize their unease at the advancement of women (and other historically underrepresented groups).

Of course, women are judged for themselves as much as men are: on their experience and their message, and their likeability. Clinton, with her baggage of investigations dating back to her husband's administration and her more recent history of email troubles, was widely seen as an imperfect messenger and therefore not deserving of the presidency. In her book *Lean In*, Google CEO Sheryl Sandberg says that women must be liked, and Clinton, polls showed, was not liked. But neither was Trump—his unfavourable rating was worse than his opponent's—yet he is president-elect.

This anomaly points to a tolerance gap in American politics when it comes to mistakes or misjudgements. In the scrupulous fact-checking that the press conducted, prompted by Trump's constant straying from the truth, Clinton was cited for roughly a fifth the number of "less than true statements" as Trump. Nonetheless he successfully branded her a "liar." A simple litmus test: put one of Trump's false statements in Clinton's mouth ("Crime is rising"; "We're the highest taxed country in the world") then ask how the voters would react.

According to Saadia Zahidi, an economist at the World Economic Forum who authors the *Gender Gap Report*, 47% of all countries have had at least one female head of state, ever. At the current rate, Zahidi has projected, it will take more than 100 years for the world to get to gender parity, where half of all heads of states are women at any given time. Will the United States get there by then?

The silver lining is that women around the world are making substantial progress in reaching highest-level offices. That progress will continue and be sustainable as more women see that it is possible and desirable.

In the United States, Gender Diversity in the Government Is Growing from the Bottom Up

Danielle Kurtzleben

In the following viewpoint, written shortly after Hillary Clinton became the first female presidential candidate of a major party, Danielle Kurtzleben explores how women are doing at other levels of government. She then goes on to discuss why there aren't more women in office even at lower levels of government, then closes with a hopeful note—though it is nowhere near parity yet, the US Congress is rapidly diversifying. Kurtzleben is a political reporter with National Public Radio, working on the network's Washington desk.

As you read, consider the following questions:

1. Why does Kurtzleben say it is "cheeky" to include president on a list comparing the percentage of women in various jobs?
2. The viewpoint references work showing that when a few women are elected to high office, there is an even greater increase in women being elected to down-ballot offices. Does this finding fit with any of the reasons women are less likely to run? If so, which one(s)?
3. Do you see in this viewpoint any of the myths that were discussed in viewpoint 1?

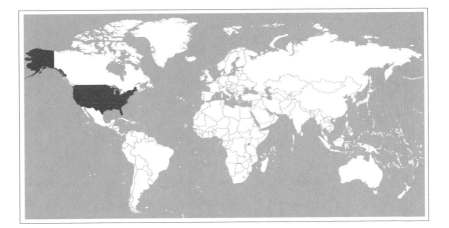

T he amendment guaranteeing women voting rights is nearly 100 years old, but women have only recently become regulars in major parties' presidential nomination fights. All those decades of slow progress culminated this year in Hillary Clinton becoming the first woman who is the presumptive nominee of a major party.

That slow creep into presidential campaigns reflects a larger trend: Women make up a bigger share of national and state lawmakers than ever, and yet the share of women in major political positions remains disproportionately low. Women make up around 19 percent of all members of Congress and less than 25 percent of all state legislators. They also make up six of the nation's 50 governors, or 12 percent.

For comparison, here's how that stacks up to a selection of other jobs in America.

From one standpoint, those are just some interesting comparisons—*Huh. Women make up about as big a share of Congress as they do the clergy.*

But there's some real perspective here. For one thing, a substantial chunk of the clergy *has* to be men. Several large American religious denominations, including Roman Catholicism, which accounts for 1 in 5 US adults, for the most part do not allow women to be ordained. Lawmaking of course has no such

Women in Government Jobs Versus Women in Other Jobs

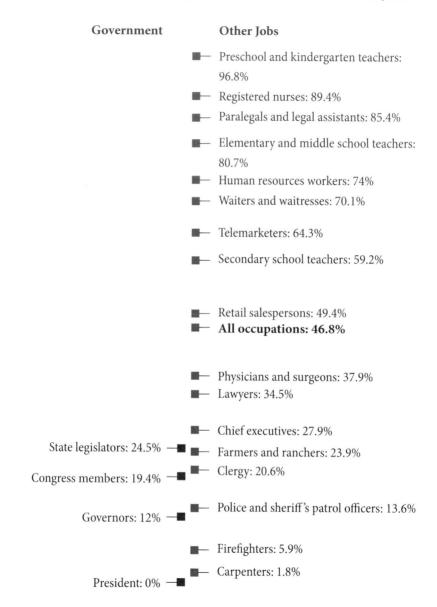

Government	Other Jobs
	Preschool and kindergarten teachers: 96.8%
	Registered nurses: 89.4%
	Paralegals and legal assistants: 85.4%
	Elementary and middle school teachers: 80.7%
	Human resources workers: 74%
	Waiters and waitresses: 70.1%
	Telemarketers: 64.3%
	Secondary school teachers: 59.2%
	Retail salespersons: 49.4%
	All occupations: 46.8%
	Physicians and surgeons: 37.9%
	Lawyers: 34.5%
	Chief executives: 27.9%
State legislators: 24.5%	Farmers and ranchers: 23.9%
Congress members: 19.4%	Clergy: 20.6%
Governors: 12%	Police and sheriff's patrol officers: 13.6%
	Firefighters: 5.9%
	Carpenters: 1.8%
President: 0%	

SOURCE: Bureau of Labor Statistics, Center for American Women and Politics, National Conference of State Legislators.

restrictions, but Congress' women's share is still stuck where it is among clergy.

Likewise, while many Americans may not think of lawmaking as a man's job, state legislators and governors are in the same neighborhood, proportion-wise, as stereotypically masculine jobs, like ranchers and cops.

And yes, it's maybe a little cheeky to put "president" on the chart, as that office will always be nonrepresentative—after all, 100 percent of the current presidents are men (and if a woman were elected, 100 percent would be women). Similarly, all of America's current presidents are black.

But then, it's also true that 100 percent of all presidents have been men, and all but one have been *white* men. The presidency has remained relatively homogenous, and it's the most prominent example of just how much women aren't involved in the highest levels of politics.

Where the Numbers Stand

The share of state legislators who were women took off starting in the 1970s, according to data from the National Conference of State Legislatures. But it has leveled off since 2010. In governors' mansions, the share of female governors spiked at 18 percent (that is, nine governors), in 2004 and 2007.

In Congress, one major spike that sticks out is 1992, the so-called Year of the Woman. In the next year's Congress, the number of women climbed from 29 to 47, and four new women also entered the Senate, bringing the total of female senators to six. (Texas Republican Kay Bailey Hutchison became a senator shortly thereafter, in June 1993, bringing the total in that Congress to seven.) Today, there are 104 women in Congress— the highest total ever, but still far lower than women's total share of the population.

Why Aren't More Women in Office?

Americans have warmed to the idea of a woman as president over the years. In the 1960s, just over half of Americans said they could vote for a woman for president, a share that rose quickly over the next few decades, according to Gallup. And in 2015, 92 percent of respondents said they'd vote for a "generally well-qualified" woman from their party, roughly similar to the share who said the same of Catholics and blacks.

That's just a poll question about women as president, but if you take it as a (rough) barometer for how Americans feel about women in political office in general, it shows that overwhelmingly, people are willing to vote for women (though there's still that 8 percent who aren't willing to vote for a woman as president).

In which case, what's keeping women out of office?

One huge issue is that women aren't getting on the ballot in the first place. In a 2012 report, American University professor of government Jennifer Lawless and Loyola Marymount University political science professor Richard Fox studied "potential candidates" of both genders—people like lawyers and activists who might reasonably get involved in politics—to determine what was keeping women from running.

They came up with seven main barriers to women running for office. In the authors' words:

1. Women are substantially more likely than men to perceive the electoral environment as highly competitive and biased against female candidates.

2. Hillary Clinton and Sarah Palin's candidacies aggravated women's perceptions of gender bias in the electoral arena. (*That is, the authors write, women saw how Clinton and Palin were treated in the 2008 election and decided not to run.*)

3. Women are much less likely than men to think they are qualified to run for office.

4. Female potential candidates are less competitive, less confident, and more risk averse than their male counterparts.

5. Women react more negatively than men to many aspects of modern campaigns.

6. Women are less likely than men to receive the suggestion to run for office—from anyone.

7. Women are still responsible for the majority of child care and household tasks.

There's evidence of that among women at both the national and state level. Female members of Congress from both parties told NPR's Tamara Keith in 2014 that women need an extra nudge (or three) before they finally decide to run for office. Women state lawmakers likewise told NPR earlier this year that they had to be talked into running.

And there's also a reinforcing element to women's lack of representation in politics that is, that women in office appear to help attract more women to office. An analysis from Obama's 2012 Analytics Director Amelia Showalter (highlighted by Vox's Matt Yglesias this week) found that electing a woman to a major office like governor or US senator today is associated with a 2 to 3 percent increase in women's representation in state legislatures four years down the road.

Showalter's findings aren't necessarily separate from Lawless and Fox's list; it's possible that if more women campaigned, other women would react less negatively to campaigning, or they might be more likely to consider themselves qualified.

There's also a partisan split in Congress; there are 22 Republicans compared to 62 Democrats in the House (by the Center for American Women in Politics' numbers) and 6 Republicans to 14 Democrats in the Senate. Why do Republican numbers remain lower than Democrats'? Polarization may be a reason, as the *New York Times'* Derek Willis wrote last year.

"A root cause of the gap is that Democratic women who are potential congressional candidates tend to fit comfortably with the liberal ideology of their party's primary voters, while many potential female Republican candidates do not adhere to the conservative ideology of their primary voters," he suggested.

Growing Diversity of All Types

Women aren't the only underrepresented group in politics. Minorities are also relatively few on the Hill—at the start of this Congress, 17 percent of members were nonwhite, compared with 38 percent of the population, according to the Pew Research Center.

Likewise, Congress is far more heavily Christian than the rest of the nation. Around 8 percent of congressional members at the start of the 114th Congress were non-Christians, compared with 27 percent of American adults, according to Pew.

Still, Congress is far more diverse than it once was, and the presence of those groups is likewise becoming more commonplace on the campaign trail. This year's massive presidential field was also remarkably diverse, including two women, two Latinos, one Jew, one Indian-American, and one African-American among the major-party candidates. (In addition, Democratic candidate Lawrence Lessig "has been vague on his personal faith," as Religion News Service reported last year.)

In India, Women Leaders Come from Political Dynasties, but That May Be Changing

Successful Lady

In many nations, particularly in Asia, that have had women leaders, those women came to power as part of a political dynasty—families whose members serve generation after generation. However, in the following excerpted viewpoint, which focuses on India, the author points out that in at least some instances, women who did not have family connections were able to rise to the top in their nations. However, these women with few exceptions still had to deal with stereotypes about women leaders and difficulties due to the prevailing religions in India.

As you read, consider the following questions:

1. How does the author define "emergency dynastic succession"?
2. The author describes how women are beginning to reach political power more legitimately through heading political parties and getting support within their own states. Do you see commonalities in this method with trends mentioned in the previous viewpoint about US women in politics?
3. In what way does the author say that Indian prime minister Indira Gandhi was an exception to the pattern discussed in this viewpoint?

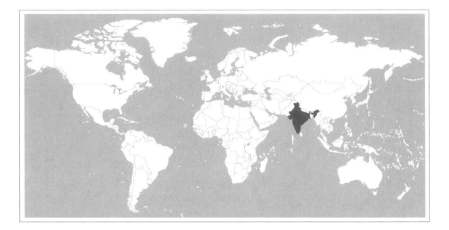

An analysis of the role of women leaders in Indian politics reveals a paradox. On the one hand, India, both in the past and at present, continues to have a number of powerful women in top political positions, well-known nationally and internationally for their strong personalities and, in some cases, efficient governance. On the other hand, the number of women in politics—in national political parties and in Parliament—continues to be woefully few. It is also alleged that the former have been able to reach top political positions mainly because they are either the daughters, or wives, of well-known political leaders. While dynastic succession of women is not absent in other parts of the world, two features seem to characterise South Asia. The first is "emergency dynastic succession" as a result of assassination or a military coup, which brought leaders such as Bandaranayake, Benazir Bhutto, Corazon Aquino or Aung San Suu Kyi to power in Sri Lanka, Pakistan, Philippines and Myanmar, respectively, gave their husbands/fathers dramatic martyrdom and provided them legitimacy (Richter, 1990: 528). The second is the dynastic continuation of a family, including its women members, over a number of generations rather than in a single instance, exerting family control over a political party, the Congress party in India providing a good example.

However, in recent years, this picture is undergoing a gradual change and an analysis of the emergence, role and impact of women political leaders reveals a more complex and nuanced picture. While the number who enter politics and reach the pinnacle remains very low, two developments point to the increasingly important role of women leaders in politics. First, the rise of political parties led by women such as Mayawati, Mamata Banerjee or Jayalalithaa, that have captured power in their own states; second, as leaders of these parties these women leaders today also occupy the national stage as regional allies that can determine the life of the central coalition in a fragmented, multi-party system. Against this backdrop, this chapter, analysing the political careers of some important women leaders, argues that while dynasty and family connections remain important variables determining entry and functioning of the large majority of women leaders in politics, a handful of women leaders have been able to enter politics on their own and emerge as independent and strong women leaders in their own right.

[...]

Role and Impact

Both Indira Gandhi and Sonia Gandhi owed their entry into politics because of their dynastic position. Subsequently, their paths have been quite different. Indira Gandhi, recognised as strong women leader, nationally and internationally, was made the prime minister by the Congress "syndicate" which felt that the party would benefit from her image as Nehru's daughter during a period when the party was facing a number of problems. Famously described by them as "goongi gudiya" (dumb doll), within a few years she was able to obtain control over the party, emerge as a strong leader and deal successfully with a number of crises: the defeat of the Congress in eight states in 1967; the Congress split in 1969, which led to the formation of the Congress (I) that obtained a parliamentary majority in 1972, based on the 20-point programme; introduction of the Green Revolution, which effectively dealt with the food crisis; and withstanding pressure from the US to introduce changes in foreign and domestic policies. She has been described as a popular plebiscitary leader, i.e. one who could appeal directly to the people and not through her party or government. However, she has faced much criticism for an authoritarian style of functioning, imposing the Emergency and trying to centralise and personalise power, which also weakened the Congress party (Hart, 1976).

Her daughter-in-law, Sonia Gandhi, who today controls the Congress, is admired on some accounts as an Italian who has adjusted to Indian life and customs and who revived an almost defunct party in the late 1990s (Kidwai, 2009). Nevertheless, she has faced criticism over the Bofors scandal, for poor administrative capacity, policy paralysis in UPA-II, and preserving the party as a family-holding by promoting her son, Rahul Gandhi, as her heir. A study argues that, unable to earn her status as a leader in her own right, "dynastic charisma" has been used as a "cover" for image-building and creating "celebrification in politics," although such manipulated attempts have limited impact as they become routinised (Chakravorti, 1999: 2842). Despite this, with her control over the Congress Party she may continue to derive support, considering the leadership vacuum in contemporary Indian politics and the emergence of Hindu fundamentalism which threatens the secular, liberal and socialist trends (ibid.: 2843). This category is not limited to Indira Gandhi and Sonia Gandhi, both of whom have enjoyed independent control of the Congress and have achievements to their credit. A younger generation of educated and capable wives and daughters are entering "feudal" political parties, which are under the control of a patriarchal figure. Good examples are the Samajwadi Party (SP), Akali Dal, NCP and the DMK, in which wives/daughters play a subordinate role.

In contrast, the seminal achievements and honest image of Sheila Dikshit, the doughty Chief Minister of Delhi, has overshadowed the fact that she is the daughter-in-law of Congress leader Uma Shankar Dikshit. During her three terms in office she has dealt effectively with factionalism within the party; been able to expand the Delhi Metro; provide a new bus transport system under the Jawaharlal Nehru National Urban Renewal Mission QNNURM); and improved roads, flyovers and other conveniences for the citizens, which have earned her much support. The rise and success of Jayalalithaa, a former film actress, is a more complicated story. While her association with popular film hero MGR enabled her to become leader of the AIADMK and the chief minister for two terms (1991–96 and 2001–06), she has also been described as a beautiful woman, a ruthless and authoritarian leader and an able administrator (Banerjee, 2004: 291). Beginning with a difficult apprenticeship under MGR, when she learned to survive in a largely male political arena, she successfully competed with V. Janaki, the widow of MGR, for control of the AIADMK, and has withstood attempts by the DMK patriarch Karunanidhi and his partymen to malign her image and misbehave with her in the Assembly. Popularly called amma, or mother, she has worked hard using an elaborate system of patronage and established herself as an independent leader (ibid.). But she still draws on MGR's charismatic, Robin Hood figure which is portrayed in her campaigns. Despite corruption charges and an opulent lifestyle, she is equated with a modern day "Tamiltaay" a uniquely Tamil ideal which appeals to men and women, combining the varied female attributes of mother, desirable woman, virginal goddess, while also personifying the Tamil language itself (Banerjee, 2004).

Despite being a Dalit woman, Mayawati has overcome tremendous opposition to become the chief minister of UP, a conservative state where Brahmin men have long enjoyed power. Selected and mentored by Kanshi Ram, when he brought her into the All India Backward and Minority Communities Employees' Federation (BAMCEF) in the mid-1980s, many felt a woman would not be able to handle the rough and tumble of Dalit politics. In the mid-1990s, hired goons of the SP, it is alleged, made an attempt on her life and person in the well-known guest house incident, but she emerged stronger from this episode (Bose, 2012). Although the BSP was established by Kanshi Ram, building a strong organisation and achieving a majority in 2007 has been her achievement. Despite her authoritarian control over the party, the cadres respect and like their Behenji. In the mid-1990s, when she became chief minister for the first time, Mayawati emerged as a role-model for Dalit women in Uttar Pradesh (Pai, 1998). During her term as chief minister from 2007 to 2012, instead of her Dalit-oriented agenda she attempted to develop backward regions and all disadvantaged sections. Nevertheless, there is also trenchant criticism that Mayawati has failed the Dalit movement by compromising with upper-caste groups/parties and is a very corrupt politician whose family members have amassed fortunes (The Indian Express, 2012).

Uma Bharati, the fiery sadhavi with oratorical skills and religious training, has sacrificed everything for her political career and is recognised as a leader of the BJP. As a sadhavi, she does not have the usual image of a woman politician; owing to her loyalty to the Sangh Parivar and Hindutva ideology, only conservative Hindu women support her, but her greatest asset is that she is perceived as a backward-caste leader. She has a number of undeniable achievements: member of the Lok Sabha for five consecutive terms, no mean achievement with no family connections and in a party not very congenial to women leaders; ministerial positions at the Centre; and vice-president of the Madhya Pradesh unit of the BJP. However, as a maverick leader, she has often challenged party rules, leading to her expulsion in 2005, forming a party of her own and eventually returning to the BJP (*Frontline*, 2005). Although viewed as honest, Bharati's record as the chief minister of Madhya Pradesh was undistinguished, leading to her replacement. She is one of the most articulate and aggressive leaders of the BJP who made her mark, not as an administrator, but by leading the party's Hindutva campaign.

Mamata Banerjee also rose without any family connections, through sheer grit and determination, to become a recognised regional and national leader. She has a number of achievements to her credit: she was elected five times to the Lok Sabha from the South Kolkata constituency; she was a Youth Congress leader in West Bengal; she formed her own party—the TMC—which is positioned as both anti-Congress and anti-Left, an ally of both the NDA and United Progressive Alliance-II (UPA-II); she was appointed railway minister in both governments. However, the most seminal achievement has been defeating the Communists who were in power for almost 30 years, a feat that could not be achieved by the Congress opposition (Banerjee, 2004). Like Jayalalithaa—a colourful and unorthodox women leader with huge public bases, flamboyant personality and "populist appeal"—Banerjee does not conform to public standards of feminine behaviour; she does not only have a reputation for unpredictability, ruthlessness, and a volatile temper, but also a mastery of the timing of public gestures, the manipulation of public sentiment, sycophantic loyalty from followers and complete control over the party. In contrast, her public image is clean; she is viewed as honest and supported by the poorer sections, especially women, although she has used both "assertive and paternalist populism" to build her constituency and gain power. Unmarried and from a modest, lower middle-class family, she still dresses in inexpensive khadi sarees and slippers and lives frugally in her old house in a congested south Kolkata area. But Banerjee has displayed little capacity to effectively govern West Bengal. Rather, she is a "street fighter" ready to gherao (ambush) political leaders, join marches and sit-ins on the streets even as chief minister, for social and political causes. Her followers compare her to the goddess Durga and a tigress for the twin qualities of female courage and intolerance for injustice, which voters find rare in politicians.

Rabri Devi, in contrast to the other women leaders studied, has commanded little respect from voters as chief minister of Bihar, except for behaving as a model wife. Put into the office by her husband Laloo Prasad Yadav, a charismatic, backward caste leader who was arrested in a fodder scam in 1997, she held the post for three successive periods: July 1997–February 1999; March 1999–2000; March 2000–05 (Sinha, 2012). Rabri Devi was able to draw on her husband's popularity and the elaborate patronage system established by him for the Yadav community. It limited her strength and ability to deal with the bureaucracy and party workers; she lost the respect of the electorate and disappeared from the political scene after the defeat of the RJD in 2005 (Spary, 2007).

Our analysis shows that, although India is a functioning democracy and has experienced considerable democratisation over the last few decades, the number of women leaders in national politics remains abysmally low. Both historical factors, which point towards slow change in patriarchal attitudes towards women and poor development of women's agency after Independence, have been responsible. Consequently, dynastic succession or family connections remain an important avenue through which women leaders have emerged. This trend is true not only of women leaders soon after Independence, but a younger generation of better-educated women—wives and daughters of established male leaders—who have, in recent years, entered Parliament and established themselves in national/state parties. Subsequently, only a few have been able to gain recognition as independent leaders; most remain in the shadow of their husbands or fathers. One reason for this is the larger phenomenon of dynastic or feudal parties in which entire families under a patriarchal figure, including women members who have a subordinate role, are involved.

The brief perusal of the functioning of some women leaders who have reached the top shows that there is no one model which fits all women leaders; rather, there are considerable differences among them on all four counts discussed. Women leaders in India are as corrupt, or as honest, as their male counterparts. Mayawati, Jayalalithaa and Sonia Gandhi are perceived by the electorate as having amassed fortunes for their family members and court cases have been filed against the first two. On the other hand, both Mamata Banerjee and Uma Bharati are viewed as honest. Some women leaders have proved highly capable in political mobilisation, establishing their own parties, maintaining a strong control over them and capturing power.

But rule by these women leaders is not always better; they have not hesitated to use authoritarian and confrontational methods, or corrupt means to achieve power, or implement desired policies.

They have also proved adept at shifting support from one coalition to another, of holding at ransom the central coalition and legislation in Parliament. Hence, leadership roles are transgendered and having more women may make no difference.

All the women leaders studied, including those who rose through dynastic succession, faced many obstacles and hardships and it took time and effort on their part to gain recognition as national leaders. Gender affects authority and women leaders— with a few exceptions such as Indira Gandhi—and commands less legitimacy, authority and respect from the electorate. Hindu imagery and stereotypes are invoked; they are seen as mother-figures, or behenji, or didi. There are different expectations from men and women, which put the latter at a distinct disadvantage making it necessary for them to work harder and prove themselves as efficient and capable in politics, even more so when in power. Failure in the case of women leads to fingers pointed at gender, but not in the case of men.

All this suggests that it is difficult for women to enter and build a career in politics in India. At the same time, in recent decades, significant changes have taken place in the states—rise in women's literacy, social movements, faster economic growth in many states, and reservation of seats for women in panchayats—which have provided a more fertile ground for women leaders in politics. In this situation, a small number of women leaders have emerged and, through sheer hard work and determination, achieved status, respect and recognition on their own. Nevertheless, this trend remains exceptional and difficult for other women to emulate. The shift from dynasty to legitimacy for women leaders has barely begun. Clearly, change is required at two levels. First, attitudes to women must change together with improvement in their economic position so that they acquire the potential to compete with men. Second, internal reforms of parties must take place so that they do not remain family concerns in which women are expected to be subordinate members with little voice of their own.

In Asia, Gender Stereotyping Actually Helps Some Women Get Elected

Mark R. Thompson

In the following viewpoint, Mark R. Thompson explores the phenomenon of women gaining power through dynasties in Asian nations other than India. Again, however, women seem to be coming to power during times when democracy is at risk. When governments are widely seen as corrupt, women, who are perceived as more virtuous and nonpolitical in this culture, have an advantage. This piece focuses on the rise of Suu Kyi in Myanmar. Thompson is director of the Southeast Asia Research Centre at the City University of Hong Kong and coeditor of Dynasties and Female Political Leaders in Asia: Gender, Power and Pedigree.

As you read, consider the following questions:

1. How does traditional religious practice inhibit the advancement of women in Myanmar, according to this viewpoint?
2. How does Thompson describe "inherited charisma," and how was that beneficial to Suu Kyi?
3. The election to high office of women in traditionally paternalistic societies is surprising. How does the author explain why that can happen without a change in the society's attitudes about women and men?

"Why Dynastic Female Leaders Win Elections in Asia," by Mark R Thompson, East Asia Forum, December 4, 2015. Reprinted by permission.

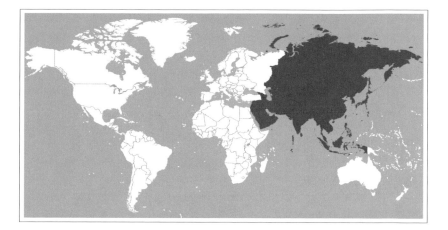

The landslide victory by Aung San Suu Kyi's National League for Democracy (NLD) party in the 8 November 2015 Myanmar election, after decades of Suu Kyi being held under house arrest, marks one of the world's most extraordinary political turnabouts.

But Suu Kyi's political ascendancy is less unique in Asia than it may at first appear. As the daughter of the country's independence leader Aung San, who was assassinated in 1947, she is only one of several prominent female dynasts—the daughters, wives or widows of "martyred" male leaders—to lead major democratic opposition movements across Asia and then assume political power. Other prominent examples are Corazon C. Aquino in the Philippines, Benazir Bhutto in Pakistan, Megawati Sukarnoputri in Indonesia, as well as Khaleda Zia and Sheikh Hasina of Bangladesh.

So why have so many dynastic female leaders emerged during democratic struggles in the region? At first glance, the success of women in politics may seem surprising because Myanmar like many other Asian countries is often seen to be patriarchal and paternalistic.

Although women played prominent political roles in pre-colonial times and during the Burmese nationalist struggle, military rule in Myanmar after 1962 drastically reduced female participation in politics.

Many women in Myanmar also lack adequate employment opportunities and have inadequate access to health care and education. Myanmar ranks relatively low (at 150 out of 187 countries) in the most recent Gender-related Development Index (GDI) rankings of the United Nations Development Programme.

Traditional religious practice is also normally seen as an obstacle for the advancement of women. In Myanmar, the discriminatory race and religion bills passed in 2015—which force women (but not men) to seek permission to marry someone from a different faith and punish adultery, thus potentially endangering women who lodge a rape accusation—are one recent example.

Yet, along with Myanmar, predominantly Buddhist countries such as Sri Lanka and Thailand have also had female dynastic leaders. Likewise there have been female dynastic leaders in the Christian Philippines and, perhaps most surprising, many predominantly Islamic countries in Asia have had women as opposition leaders who later became heads of government.

What then explains the success of female politicians in Asia?

The case of Aung San Suu Kyi and other dynastic female leaders in Asia shows that gender stereotyping can sometimes prove to be a political plus in a crisis situation. As a woman Suu Kyi could be portrayed as non-political—a virtuous alternative to the country's corrupt, Machiavellian military leaders that have ruled since the 1988 anti-military protests.

Women have also, perhaps counterintuitively, benefited from their association with the family. Suu Kyi, like other dynastic female leaders, promised to cleanse the soiled public realm with private, familial virtue. Suu Kyi is often called "sister Suu" by her supporters. Other female leaders have similarly been called "aunts" or "mothers." Suu Kyi's courage in the face of repression, tenaciousness over decades of opposition and eloquence in criticising military rule further increased this "moral capital."

The choice of Suu Kyi as opposition leader was also advantageous as she acquired what the German sociologist Max Weber called "inherited charisma." A male dynast successor is more likely to be judged on his own merits, making it more difficult for him to inherit the mantle of charisma from a father or brother to whom he may be compared unfavourably. But a widow, wife or daughter is often seen to better embody their husbands' or fathers' charisma.

Suu Kyi's "national inheritance" enabled her to keep the military regime on the defensive for decades.

The examples of female dynastic leaders in power elsewhere in Asia also points to some particular problems that Suu Kyi may face in the near future. Male opponents are likely to try to portray her as a "weak woman." The NLD coalition may face fragmentation after she leaves the political scene unless she is able to adequately institutionalise her legacy. At least parts of the military may try to challenge her hold on power, as they did Corazon Aquino's in the Philippines or Benazir Bhutto's in Pakistan.

Suu Kyi will also have to face up to the challenge of ethnic and religious divisions in Myanmar. During Myanmar's recent political liberalisation and the election campaign, ethno-chauvinist forces emerged, particularly among hard-line Buddhist monks who fanned hatred of the Rohingya minority and used anti-Muslim rhetoric.

Many human rights activists have criticised Suu Kyi for not speaking up to defend the Rohingya and for not running a single Muslim candidate on the NLD slate. The NLD's strategy has been to keep the focus on their democratic opposition to years of military rule, while largely ignoring this religious strife. With the election won and power tantalisingly close, it remains to be seen whether Aung San Suu Kyi becomes more outspoken on injustices perpetrated against the Rohingya or takes action to counter general anti-Muslim sentiments.

It is still uncertain whether Suu Kyi can actually translate the NLD's electoral victory into democratic civilian rule after more than a half century of military dictatorship. But to have gotten this far against very long odds is in large part due to the qualities of moral leadership she inherited and further built upon as a female dynastic leader.

Periodical and Internet Sources Bibliography

The following articles have been selected to supplement the diverse views presented in this chapter

Molly Bangs, "Women's Underrespresentation in Politics: No, It's Not Just an Ambition Gap," Century Foundation, September 21, 2017. https://tcf.org/content/commentary /womens-underrepresentation-politics-no-not-just-ambition -gap/?session=1.

Hannah Beech, "What Happened to Myanmar's Human Rights Icon?," *New Yorker*, October 2, 2017. https://www.newyorker .com/magazine/2017/10/02/what-happened-to-myanmars -human-rights-icon.

Alexander Burns, "What Happens When Multiple Women Run for President? Democrats Are Starting to Find Out," *Seattle Times*, updated October 19, 2018. https://www.seattletimes.com/nation -world/nation-politics/what-happens-when-multiple-women -run-for-president-democrats-are-starting-to-find-out.

Jeff Desjardins, "How Gender Diversity Enhances Society," World Economic Forum, February 5, 2018. https://www.weforum.org /agenda/2018/02/how-gender-diversity-enhances-society.

Kathy Gilsinan, "The Myth of 'Female' Foreign Policy," *Atlantic*, August 25, 2016. https://www.theatlantic.com/international /archive/2016/08/-foreign-policy-clinton-may-thatcher-women -leadership/497288.

Matthew Qvortrup, "How Angela Merkel's Unspoken Feminism Transformed German Politics," *New Statesman America*, March 5, 2018. https://www.newstatesman.com/world/europe/2018/03 /how-angela-merkel-s-unspoken-feminism-transformed -german-politics.

Alexandra Svokos, "Justin Trudeau Explained His Gender-Balanced Cabinet," Elite Daily, April 6, 2017. https://www.elitedaily.com /news/politics/justin-trudeau-talks-feminist-cabinet/1853014.

GLOBAL VIEWPOINTS

Sexism and
Gender Diversity
in Government

In the United States, Systemic Gender Discrimination Stands in the Way of Electing a Female President

Rice University

When Hillary Clinton lost the 2016 presidential election, experts and voters alike were stunned by the outcome. Since then, there have been many theories about why this happened. Sexism is far from the most discussed possibility, yet sexism clearly played a role in the election. In the following viewpoint, authors from Rice University argue that Clinton's loss was likely due not just to the sexist comments made by Trump and his supporters but to something much more difficult to address: systemic gender discrimination within US culture.

As you read, consider the following questions:

1. How do Corrington and Hebl define sexism, according to this viewpoint?
2. What do the authors mean by "agentic behavior," and how might that have hurt Hillary Clinton?
3. What steps do Corrington and Hebl suggest for getting the United States ready for a female president?

"Op-Ed Says Clinton May Have Lost Election Due to 'Systemic Gender Discrimination,'" Phys.org, March 21, 2018.

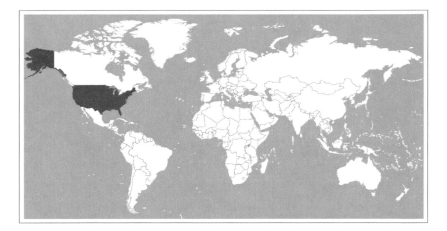

Despite being described by former US President Barack Obama as the most-qualified presidential nominee in US history, former Secretary of State Hillary Clinton lost the 2016 campaign for the highest office in the land. That outcome may have been the result of systemic gender discrimination, according to psychologists at Rice University.

Authors Abby Corrington, a Rice psychology Ph.D. student, and Mikki Hebl, the Martha and Henry Malcolm Lovett Chair of Psychology in Rice's School of Social Sciences, drew upon existing psychological research to offer possible explanations for Clinton's loss. Their op-ed, "America Clearly Isn't Ready for a Female President: Why?," will appear in an upcoming edition of *Equality, Diversity and Inclusion: An International Journal*.

"We ultimately decided to focus on this topic to discuss how gender may have influenced the 2016 election, and what that means for us moving forward," Corrington said. "We wanted to discuss the theoretical reasons for the 2016 election outcome."

The researchers outlined four gender-related theories that they believe serve as possible explanations for why Clinton fell short in the election, and they offered suggestions for future female candidates.

Sexism

According to Corrington and Hebl, sexism—defined as prejudice, stereotyping or discrimination on the basis of sex—can take a variety of forms, as exemplified by the theory of ambivalent sexism. Ambivalent sexism comprises two subgroups of sexism: hostile sexism, which reflects overtly negative evaluations and stereotypes about a gender (for example, the ideas that women are incompetent and inferior to men), and benevolent sexism, which represents evaluations of gender that may appear subjectively positive (for example, the belief that women can and should rely on men for protection) but are actually more broadly damaging to people and gender equality.

"Women are frequently subtyped into different categories, such as housewives, career women, babes and feminists," Corrington said. "Hostile sexism is usually directed toward women who challenge men's power and traditional gender roles, whereas benevolent sexism is typically reserved for women who endorse male power and traditional gender roles."

Corrington said that given the research on the negative views toward nontraditional women (such as career women and feminists), it should come as no surprise that, since Clinton is perhaps the quintessential nontraditional "career woman," she would be subject to ambivalent (and often overt) sexism, rendering her election to the presidency unlikely.

Social Role Theory

Social role theory suggests that the principal cause of sex-based differences in social behavior is the distribution of men and women into distinct social roles and with different associated behaviors, Corrington and Hebl said.

"Men in the US tend to be more prevalent in positions of power, such as in business and politics," Corrington said. "And traditionally, women in the US have been the homemakers and caregivers. Even as women have entered the workforce, they tend to receive lower salaries, converge in certain occupations and rarely occupy the highest levels of organizational hierarchies. The combination of the gender-based division of labor and the fact that women have less power, lower status and fewer resources than men in most societies is the underlying cause of gender-based differences in social behavior.

"Women are known traditionally for displaying communal (interpersonally facilitative, friendly) behaviors, while men are characterized for their displays of agentic (independent, assertive) behaviors," she said. "Research shows that when men, and especially women, deviate from these expected behaviors, they face backlash."

Corrington said that Clinton's display of agentic behavior as she sought what is arguably the most powerful leadership position in the world could explain her negative evaluation by voters.

Stereotype Content Model

Stereotype content model is a theory that group stereotypes and interpersonal impressions form along two dimensions: warmth and competence. Corrington said that individuals from out-groups (social groups with which the perceiver does not identify) are rarely seen as high in both warmth and competence and that positive stereotypes on one dimension act jointly with negative stereotypes on the other dimension to maintain the advantage of the more privileged group.

She said that traditionally, subgroups of women such as career-oriented women and female athletes are viewed as competent but not warm, and groups such as housewives and "chicks" are viewed as warm but not competent.

While one might imagine that a career woman engaged in the highest-status competition in the nation would be perceived as low in warmth and high in competence, Corrington said, this was not entirely true.

"Despite the description of Hillary Clinton by former President Barack Obama as 'the most-qualified candidate' to ever pursue the presidency, it seems this sentiment was not shared as broadly as his statement suggests, meaning that Clinton was not able to enjoy the usual benefit of being perceived as a 'career woman,'" she said. "Not only was she perceived as lacking warmth, but due to a series of incidents such as use of a private network server, leaked DNC emails and 'flip-flopping' on issues, she was also perceived as lacking competence."

Corrington said that the irony in how Clinton was perceived was that Donald Trump had no experience in politics or foreign policy, but was elected president.

"This is a clear example of men and women being judged according to different standards," she said. "And a possible explanation for the different standards is that overall, individuals are used to seeing men in positions of power, which could be why voters were more likely to look past perceptions of low competence for Donald Trump than they were for Hillary Clinton."

System Justification Theory

System justification theory proposes that people have several underlying needs, which vary from individual to individual, that can be satisfied by the defense and justification of the status quo, even when it may be disadvantageous to certain people, Corrington and Hebl said.

Corrington said that previous psychology research suggests that humans have a fundamental desire to reduce uncertainty, threat and social discord. One study in particular found that when white Americans whose ethnicity is a central aspect of their identity—regardless of whether they were Democrats or Republicans—were reminded of the fact that members of nonwhite racial groups will become the demographic majority in the US by 2042, they expressed greater concern about the declining status and influence of white Americans, increased support for Trump and anti-immigration policies and increased their resistance to political correctness.

Corrington said this finding from previous research is a good example of how the system justification theory played out in the 2016 election.

"When white individuals were reminded that members of their race would be outnumbered by members of other races, they reacted strongly against that notion by supporting Trump and policies that they thought would reinforce their dominance, even if those policies may be disadvantageous to some people," Corrington said. "Voters may have perceived Clinton's political platform as one that would be threatening to this dominance."

As indicated by the title of their op-ed, Corrington and Hebl concluded that America is not ready for a woman president, and they suggested the following four solutions, guided by each of the previously discussed theories, to assure that the next qualified female candidate gets a fair shot at the presidency.

- More women must get into politics. Politics cannot be seen as a man's sphere only; there must be more female exemplars, and they must be distributed throughout the political spectrum—from city councils to oval offices.

- People must be more aware of not only the overt sexism they harbor and express but also the ambivalent sexism they hold.

- People must be more aware of the stereotype content model and how people judge men and women according to different standards.

- Men must understand that the placement of women in positions of power does not displace them.

"The election of Donald Trump to the presidency is an indication that we have a long way to go before we see a female president," Corrington and Hebl said. "But our hope is that Nov. 8, 2016, and the years that follow are simply the soil in which the seeds of change are being planted."

In Australia, Sexism in Politics Could Make Women Hesitant to Run for Office

Avery Poole

The United States is not the only nation where overt sexism finds its way into politics. In the following viewpoint, Dr. Avery Poole discusses an incident on the floor of the Australian Parliament in which a male senator lodged a shocking sexist slur at one of his (few) female colleagues. The author argues that the most effective way to stop this kind of unacceptable behavior is to elect more women. Poole is assistant director of the Melbourne School of Government in Melbourne, Australia.

As you read, consider the following questions:

1. According to the author, what would have been the consequences had Senator David Leyonhjelm made such comments about a female coworker in the business, rather than the political, world?
2. What are the risks, according to Poole, of allowing this kind of behavior in government and politics?
3. What solutions to this problem does the author suggest?

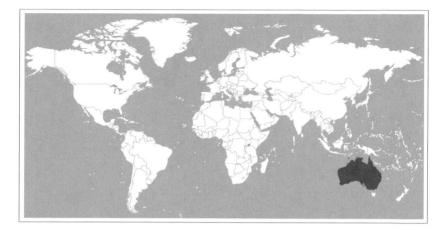

The sexist slur Senator David Leyonhjelm unapologetically dished out to Senator Sarah Hanson-Young on the floor of the nation's parliament would be unacceptable in the average Australian work place.

Not only would it be unacceptable, Senator Leyonhjelm could expect to be facing serious disciplinary action from his employer.

But there is no "employer" in parliament to reprimand Senator Leyonhjelm for his sexist abuse and defend Hanson-Young's right to a safe workplace. Instead, it is fought out repeatedly in the glare of the media—the slur rehashed for public consumption as Senator Leyonhjelm refuses to apologise for what Hanson-Young has rightly called out as sexist bullying.

And amid the fallout it is clear that sexist abuse like this in parliament is commonplace. As former Liberal party staffer Paula Matthewson wrote "this white noise of abuse isn't picked up by the chamber microphones, but it can be deafening to those who are actually in the room."

Why then would a talented and skilled woman want to subject herself to such contemptible behaviour?

The big danger of episodes like this is that women will continue to be dissuaded from even trying to run for office. We urgently need more women in parliament if we are to be a more representative and diverse democracy, but the catch-22 is that to change the culture of politics and encourage women to run, we need more women to already be in politics.

Australia's representation of women in parliament is poor by international standards.

Only 31 per cent of Australian Federal parliamentarians are female and the Inter-Parliamentary Union ranks Australia down at 50th in the world for female representation; behind many Scandinavian, African and Latin American countries that boast over 40 per cent representation in their lower houses. The likes of New Zealand, France, Spain, Germany and the UK are all doing better than us.

Some of this outperformance reflects quota systems, whether voluntary and compulsory in some countries. But Cuba at 53 per cent women, Finland at 42 per cent, and Denmark at 37 per cent, don't have quotas.

It is also the case that electoral systems that rely more on proportional representation are more likely to elect women. According to the IPU, proportional systems incentivise parties to broaden their appeal by including women candidates on their lists but it can be harder to break the dominance of men in single-member constituencies. For example, proportional representation in the senate has delivered a chamber that is 38 per cent women, but a lower house that's just 27 per cent female.

The key challenge here is better supporting women to run in the first place. The evidence in Australia suggests that when women do run they do stand a good chance of success.

But as the experience of Hanson-Young highlights, women face a double standard when it comes to the increased scrutiny placed on politicians. As the experiences of political leaders like Julia Gillard, Hilary Clinton and former Canadian Prime Minister Kim Campbell demonstrate, women in politics tend to be judged more harshly simply because they are women. The marital status of female politicians, and whether they have children, are all subject to comment and debate in a way that men are rarely subjected to.

The IPU has also noted that as more women enter parliaments around the world, they are being met by increased harassment and aggression. This may include not just demeaning messages in the media and on social media, but also threats of murder, kidnapping and beatings. There are instances of women MPs having their microphones simply turned off to stop them from being heard.

Those who claim that women need to somehow "toughen up" completely miss the point that the going is simply tougher. The fact that women face a disproportionately heavier weight of deeply personal scrutiny compared to men is clearly a disincentive for women to make a go of politics.

This is why we need explicit initiatives to help prepare more talented women to go through with their aspirations to serve and make a difference.

In the US, the John F. Kennedy School of Government at Harvard runs a successful program that aims to help prepare women to take a tilt at office whether local, state or federal government. Inspired by the US program, the Melbourne School of Government at the University of Melbourne is into the third year of its own nonpartisan Pathways to Politics Program for Women.

The program, which is limited to 25 places each year (there were 140 applications in 2017), brings together women with serious aspirations to serve, with women who have been there and still are there; whether as politicians, political party operators or political journalists. Last year speakers included Peta Credlin, Penny Wong, and Bridget McKenzie.

The focus is on providing skills and experience in networking, speech-making, navigating political machineries and the media, ethics, polling and campaigning. It aims to foster tight bonds around mentoring and support, which are critical for sustained careers.

So, why does this matter?

If parliament is to be truly representative and if the burning issues affecting people's everyday lives are to be properly heard then we need a diverse parliament, and that includes more women, just as it includes having people from different backgrounds whether that be ethnicity, regionality, social-economic status, sexuality or profession.

A more diverse parliament will change the behaviour inside parliament.

Women are easy targets as a minority, but that will change as more women enter parliament. The more diverse the parliament the more respectful it will become, and hopefully, a more respectful parliament will put the focus more on policy and the hard work politicians do, rather than personal attacks.

But it isn't just about getting more women into parliament because they are women. By opening up the opportunity to more women we can cast the net a lot wider so that we attract the really talented and passionate people who should be representing us in elected office.

At times like this, when the sexism inside politics is exposed in the raw, there will always be worries that the committed and talented women we need will be put off.

But thankfully today, the behaviour of Senator Leyonhjelm will, if anything, be igniting a fire in the belly of women to push ahead anyway and change the conversation.

In the United States, Women Candidates Often Struggle to Win Over Female Voters

Peggy Drexler

In the following viewpoint, Peggy Drexler considers the question of why female voters are often unwilling to vote for female candidates. She cites reports suggesting that women are often less likely than men to vote for female candidates. The author explores several possible reasons for this before pointing out that things are improving. Drexler is an assistant professor of psychology at Weill Medical College of Cornell University and author of Our Fathers Ourselves: Daughters, Fathers, and the Changing American Family.

As you read, consider the following questions:

1. What sorts of double standards between men and women does Drexler mention in this piece?
2. What are some of the reasons that women behave as if they really don't want equality, according to the viewpoint?
3. This viewpoint was written in 2013. Do you think the points made here still apply after the elections of 2016 and 2018? Why or why not?

M any reports still show that female voters remain reluctant to vote for a woman. In an AP analysis of data from the

2006 American National Election Study Pilot Test, researchers found that when it came to selecting a candidate for president, gender matters more for women than for men. And that while women are more likely to vote for a candidate because she is female, they are also more likely to dismiss her for that very same reason.

Back in August, the ever-charming Fox News suggested this was because women voters "want a Daddy figure." Others point to a resistance against feminism, and a sense that women are themselves holding fast to the paternalistic view that they are not as good as men. Sherrye Henry wrote *The Deep Divide* after her own unsuccessful bid for a New York senate seat. In it, she argues that women won't support female political candidates because of the disparity between what women believe and their willingness to act on those beliefs—the "deep divide." That is, women say they want equality, but do they really?

The truth is that double standards still exist between women and men in positions of power, and female candidates are often asked to be not only as qualified and appealing as their male counterparts, but far more so. Tiffany Dufu, president of the White House Project, a nonprofit organization committed to increasing female leadership in politics and elsewhere, has said that female voters are indeed tougher on female candidates and that, in fact, "any individual who does not fit the leadership status quo—a man, and usually a privileged, white one has to meet a higher bar." The same divergent expectations for women versus men show up in other fields, such as medicine, where a male surgeon may be the preferred choice unless, of course, his female counterpart graduated the top of her Ivy League class, has an impeccable track record and selective patient list, and is otherwise unimpeachable.

Women, still judge other women—simply put, continue to be judged against the standards initiated and maintained by men. And because many women therefore know quite well what it's like to feel judged, they then turn that judgment back on one another. Women are notoriously harsh towards other women, especially in the professional sense. According to a recent study by the

Quotas Might Help Increase Female Participation in the UK Government

This month, a three-year study by researchers at the University of Pittsburgh suggested a reason women are less likely to go into politics: they do not like going through the election process. It's not so surprising, really—who but the most thick-skinned would willingly go through a cycle that so closely scrutinises female politicians' fashion choices, sexual pasts and even their childcare arrangements?

The advantages of a diverse parliament cannot be overstated—at least until we get one that more closely resembles the society it purports to represent and serve. It's not just on gender that the house is falling down: the problem is intersectional, covering other factors such as class and race. Westminster has an ethnicity imbalance, and research by the *Guardian* into the backgrounds of candidates for 2015 suggests that Labour and the Lib Dems are choosing more from the political classes, while the Tories' candidates are mostly male, and from the worlds of business and finance. More than one-third of MPs elected in 2010 attended fee-paying schools (the figure in the general adult population is less than 10%). The relative lack of women is yet another black mark against the "mother of parliaments."

The UN has identified different ways to increase the participation of women in politics, among them the introduction of quotas and marshalling grassroots community organisations to empower women. In Rwanda, there are legislated quotas at every level of politics, resulting in a lower house in which women occupy 51 of the 80 seats. In that regard, the small east-African country is ahead of such bastions of gender equality as Iceland and Finland (numbers 1 and 2 respectively in the WEF report). Women-only shortlists have been a Labour mainstay for close to a generation—and the party has 86 female MPs (31%) in parliament. The Tories are at 16% women; the Lib Dems at 12%. It's clearly not the only way, but it is one that has palpable results.

"What Can We Do to Improve Female Representation in Politics?" by Bim Adewunmi, Guardian News and Media Limited, December 15, 2014.

Workplace Bullying Institute, women bully other women at work—verbal abuse, job sabotage, misuse of authority, and destroying of relationships—more than 70 percent of the time. Another study by Business Environment found 72 percent of women judged female coworkers based on what they wore to the office.

None of this is helped by Hollywood, which continues to perpetuate the notion of the "career" (ever hear of the "career" man) woman as a bitchy, unwomanly, Prada-wearing devil. Many of these movies, marketed largely to women, depict powerful women as, at best, something to be wary of, and at worst, something to disdain. Women want to like their female candidates. In the voting booths, do they want to support the tough, demanding boss lady they'd never invite over for dinner? Or the nurturing, motherly softy who'd get creamed on the Senate floor? Can a woman ever be both? Can she be neither? Unfortunately it's been hard to convince voters that women aren't necessarily one or the other: good at their jobs or likable.

Of course, women's resistance to female candidates could also be owing to how she looks. It's pointless to argue that looks don't matter. In her groundbreaking 1999 book, *Survival of the Prettiest*, Harvard Medical School psychologist Nancy Etcoff argued that good-looking people get better jobs, are better paid, and have an easier time in life. Evolutionarily speaking, pretty people win. Science confirms this as it relates to politics: A 2006 study from the University of Helsinki looked at the role of beauty in politics and found that the better-looking the candidate, the more competent, trustworthy, and likeable he or she was perceived to be.

The study also looked at male candidates, but again, the stakes are higher for women, who are judged if they're unattractive and then judged if they do something about it. Just look at Nancy Pelosi: Bright-eyed in her early 70s, the "glamorous grandma"—as the press have dubbed her in articles that continue to focus nearly as much on her face as on her politics—has endured ridicule for preternaturally dewy skin and eyebrows that seem ever on the rise. Oh, and that she wears too much makeup. Hillary Clinton, meanwhile, has hair watchdogs monitoring her every straightening. She is one of the most accomplished politicians of the century, but her choice of hair accessories—scrunchie or headband?—is still hotly debated. Her longtime hair stylist even got a book deal.

The good news is that Americans—men and women—are becoming more conditioned to the notion of female power, from the victories of Election 2012 to the Pentagon's recently-lifted ban on women in combat. With every move toward equality, women in charge will no longer be seen as an aberration, a fluke, rarities to be examined and analyzed like specimens.

In the United States, Views About Women in Politics Depend on Gender

D'Vera Cohn and Gretchen Livingston

In the following viewpoint, published just under six months before the 2016 US presidential election, D'Vera Cohn and Gretchen Livingston explore the views of Americans regarding female political leaders. Perhaps somewhat surprisingly, large majorities of both genders said they thought women and men made equally good political leaders. However, the devil is in the details, and here opinions about those details vary a great deal, depending on whether the respondent is male or female. Cohn is a senior writer and editor at Pew Research Center. Livingston is a senior researcher with Pew.

As you read, consider the following questions:

1. According to this survey, what is the major reason American women say that there aren't more women in politics?
2. What advantages did women in this survey see in having women as political leaders?
3. Do you think any of these opinions have changed since this survey was conducted?

"Americans' Views of Women as Political Leaders Differ by Gender," by D'Vera Cohn and Gretchen Livingston, Pew Research Center, May 19, 2016.

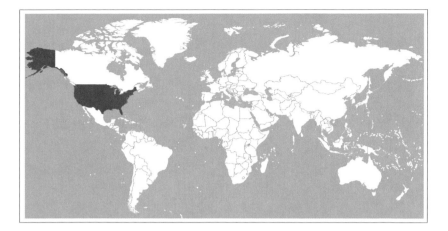

For the first time in history, a woman is the leading candidate for the presidential nomination of a major US political party. As Democrat Hillary Clinton wages her campaign to be the first female chief executive, what do Americans have to say in general about the prospects and qualifications of female candidates for high political offices?

For the most part, Americans—including similar shares of men (74%) and women (76%)—said in a 2014 Pew Research Center survey that women and men make equally good political leaders. When it comes to essential traits of a leader, both men and women saw women as being more compassionate, organized and honest than men, and saw men as being more ambitious and decisive (though for most traits, an even higher share said both genders possess them equally). But the survey found marked differences between women and men on other questions relating to gender and leadership, including the reasons that more women have not been elected. Here are five key findings from the survey on gender differences in views about women and leadership:

1. Women More Likely to Say It's Easier for Men to Get Elected

Women in our survey said men had an easier path to political leadership, and they also were more likely to say that having more female leaders would improve the quality of life for women. About three-quarters (73%) of women said it's easier for men to get elected to high political office, while 58% of men agreed. And 38% of women said that having more women in top political or business leadership positions would improve the quality of life for all women "a lot." Only half as many men (19%) agreed. There were similar differences by political party on this question, with more than twice as many Democrats (39%) as Republicans (17%) saying that having more women in high political office would improve the lives of women, while independents (28%) ranked in the middle.

2. Why Aren't More Women in Top Elective Office?

In 2015, there were 104 women in Congress, a record number representing 19% of all Senate and House seats. There was no overall consensus among the public in our survey on what holds women back from gaining top elective offices, though women were far more likely than men to cite societal and institutional factors as major reasons. About half (47%) of women said that a major reason there are not more women in top political offices is that female candidates are held to higher standards than men, compared with 28% of men who said so. Four-in-ten women (41%), compared with three-in-ten men (31%), said that a major reason for the lack of women in top political offices is that many Americans aren't ready to elect a woman to a higher office. And 33% of women, compared with 21% of men, said that females getting less support from party leaders is a major reason. Relatively small shares of men (15%) and women (18%) said that family responsibilities are a major reason that fewer women hold elective offices.

3. Women See Advantages to Female Political Leadership

There was a wide and consistent gender gap in opinions about the relative strengths of male and female political leaders on five attributes tested in our survey, though most men and women said there is no gender difference on these traits. One of the largest gender gaps was on the ability to work out compromises: 41% of women compared with 27% of men said women are better at this. Women also were more likely than men to say female leaders surpass men in being honest and ethical, working to improve quality of life for Americans, standing up for their beliefs despite political pressure, and being persuasive. The survey also asked about gender differences among leaders on various policy issues, and found less-pronounced differences among male and female respondents.

4. Generational Differences Among Women in Our Survey on the Attributes That a Woman Brings to Political Office

Younger women were less likely to give female leaders an edge over male leaders, and instead were more likely to say men and women are equally likely to possess certain traits. For example, when it comes to working out compromises, 33% of Millennial women and 37% of Generation X women said women are better than men, compared with about half of women from the Baby Boomer (47%) and Silent (50%) generations who said so. Asked about which gender is better at working to improve Americans' quality of life, only 22% of Millennial women and 24% of Gen X women said female leaders are better, compared with 39% of Baby Boomer women and 35% of Silent generation women who said so.

5. Democrats More Enthused than Republicans About a Potential Female President

In November 2014, before Clinton had declared her candidacy, Democrats were more enthused than Republicans about a potential female president. This partisan difference was bigger than the gender difference among survey respondents. Our survey question asked people whether they hoped a female president will be elected in their lifetime, or whether that did not matter to them. For many, the prospect of a Clinton presidency may have influenced their responses to this "hypothetical" question. Democratic women (69%) were the most likely to say they hoped a female US president would be elected in their lifetimes, followed by Democratic men (46%) and independent women (45%). Among Republicans, fewer women (20%) and men (16%) said they hoped for this, as did about a third (32%) of independent men.

VIEWPOINT 5

In the United States, Implicit Sexism Affected the Presidential Election

Daniel Bush

In the following excerpted viewpoint published just before the 2016 US presidential election, Daniel Bush visits with several white American men to gauge how they feel about the possibility of a female president. Though their attitudes and opinions differ, it is clear that this is a demographic Clinton—and to a lesser degree, any female candidate—would have trouble winning over. Of course Clinton ended up losing the election to Donald Trump. Bush is digital politics editor and senior writer for PBS NewsHour.

As you read, consider the following questions:

1. What problems did Clinton have with white male voters, according to the author?
2. How long have white men been abandoning the Democratic Party, according to this viewpoint?
3. This viewpoint suggests that Clinton's loss would be at least in part due to white men not being able to vote for her because she is a woman. Do you agree?

A rmando Manno was in a good mood. His bartending shift at Louie's Bar & Grill in Akron, Ohio was almost over, and the Cleveland Cavaliers were ahead in the first quarter of a pivotal playoff game. It was May 25, near the end of the primary season,

"The Hidden Sexism That Could Sway the Election," by Daniel Bush, Public Broadcasting Service (PBS), 2016. Reprinted by permission.

and talk had shifted to the presidential election. "Trump is going to make the right moves," Manno, the son of Italian immigrants and a lifelong Republican, said as he wiped down the bar. "You don't become a gazillionaire if you don't know what you're doing. He's gotta have something upstairs." As for Hillary Clinton, Manno said that he didn't want her in the White House. She was untrustworthy and willing to say anything to get elected, he said. And she possessed another, more fundamental shortcoming, Manno added: her gender. "Nothing against women," he said, "but I don't want a woman president right now."

Manno laughed and gave a sheepish, that's-just-how-I-feel shrug. As he turned away, a waitress named Mary Stone quietly offered a different point of view. Though she's also planning to vote for Trump in the fall, Stone said she could relate to the cultural barriers that Clinton faces as a woman. "Men are still chauvinistic enough to think that women can't do the same job as them. And I think that's an issue."

Heading into the general election, Clinton has a wide lead over Donald Trump among minority and female voters. But Clinton, who made history last week as the first woman to clinch the nomination of a major US party, has struggled with the one big voting bloc that's truly up for grabs in 2016: moderate white men. White men also happen to be Trump's base. If he doesn't get a record number of them to turn out, it's hard to see how he wins the presidency. Women, African-Americans, and Latinos will still play a crucial role in the race. They skew Democratic and anti-Trump. If Clinton keeps that coalition together, she can afford to lose some white men. But she can't afford to lose too many.

The Clinton campaign knows this. Clinton spent significant time in the primaries courting white male voters—in particular white, mostly working-class men in the key Rust Belt and Midwestern swing states that usually decide presidential elections. And yet, despite all the effort, the results were abysmal. Clinton lost the overall male vote to Bernie Sanders by an average of 10 points in Pennsylvania, Ohio, Iowa and Wisconsin, according to an analysis of exit poll data. She also lost men by double-digits in states as varied as Nevada, Connecticut and Oklahoma. In contrast, she won the male vote by wide margins in states that have large numbers of African-American and Latino voters. In short, white men are the last holdout.

Female candidates have long faced more resistance, and received less support from men and women alike, even though the percentage of people who say they feel comfortable voting for women has gone steadily up. In 1937, just 33 percent of Americans said they would vote for a female presidential candidate, according to Gallup's first poll on the subject. By 2015, that number had climbed to 92 percent. But giving a non-sexist answer to a pollster is easy enough; the country has almost aced that test. Actually voting for a female presidential candidate has proven to be a much bigger challenge.

Obviously, gender isn't the only factor contributing to Clinton's struggles with white male voters. She has real shortcomings, like any male or female candidate. They were evident in her failure to put Sanders away early on in the primaries. Her national approval ratings are remarkably low for a presidential nominee, and part of that can be traced to men and women across the political spectrum who have legitimate policy disagreements with Clinton (though her likeability numbers are gendered as well; and of course some women hold subconscious biases towards female candidates, too). White men began abandoning the Democratic Party in the 1960s, for reasons that had nothing to do with gender. The trend accelerated under Ronald Reagan and shows no signs of slowing today.

Still, social science evidence, primary exit polls and my interviews with researchers and dozens of voters indicate that white men's attitudes toward Clinton are driven by a complex mix of conscious and subconscious sexism. "The gender issue, people say it shouldn't matter anymore," said Nancy Mills, a member of the Democratic National Committee and longtime powerbroker in Pennsylvania politics. "But it always matters because it exists. You can't ignore it and make it go away."

Social psychology research tells us that everyone thinks they're not prejudiced, and everyone is wrong. We all have built-in biases, whether we recognize them or not. I spoke to white men across Pennsylvania and Ohio last month for this story—Democrats and Republicans, old men and young guys, middle class professionals and blue-collar workers. They all insisted that they weren't sexist. Nevertheless, many said they were uncomfortable with the thought of a female president.

"Bias in general, whether it's directed at gender, race, or anything else, is more automatic than people think," said Susan Fiske, a leading researcher on prejudice and stereotypes who teaches at Princeton University. "And it's also more ambivalent than we realize. So that makes it harder to detect in ourselves."

I should say here that my goal is not to mansplain the way that sexism works to people who already get it. Rather, it's to work through a thorny issue at the heart of this election that many men, like myself, probably haven't spent as much time thinking about as we should. We don't have to if we don't want to, which is just one of many unfair privileges that come with being a man.

It can be easy to think of bias and racism in absolute terms. You're either racist or you're not. But actually, it's not that simple.

The theory of ambivalent sexism, more than anything else, helps illustrate men's subconscious bias against Clinton, but it's hard to understand—at least it was for me—because it clashes with many people's ideas about prejudice. It can be easy to think of bias and racism in absolute terms. You're either racist or you're not. The same thinking applied to gender up until the mid-1990s. That's when Fiske, working with Peter Glick, a social psychologist at Lawrence University in Appleton, Wisconsin, published a breakthrough paper that laid out their ambivalent sexism theory. The theory, which has since been accepted by researchers around the world, helped form the basis for how experts study sexism today. Fiske and Glick separated sexism into two distinct categories. The first kind, known as "hostile" sexism, encompasses overtly negative views about women. It's what we usually associate with gender discrimination. The second kind, known as "benevolent" sexism, describes positive attitudes and actions which men take toward women that are based, deep-down, in feelings of superiority and dominance.

"Men have ambivalent attitudes toward women that are prejudiced and paternalistic, but that are also based on love and interdependence," Glick said. In other words, we can say we like women and really mean it while also harboring a combination of conflicting biases that we don't even realize exist. If that sounds confusing, it's because it is. For any male readers out there who might want to grapple with this some more: the next time you offer to carry your wife or girlfriend or female friend's heavy shopping bag, or go on a drive with a member of the opposite sex and insist on doing all of the driving, try and honestly break down the gender dynamic. Sure, you mean well. But it may not be that simple.

When it comes to politics and the 2016 presidential election, hostile sexism plays out in obvious ways. We have Trump to thank for that. He has insulted the physical appearance of Carly Fiorina, his lone female primary opponent ("Look at that face. Would anyone vote for that?"), and attacked FOX News host Megyn

Kelly ("She had blood coming out of her wherever") after Kelly highlighted his long track record of misogynist comments at a Republican debate. The list goes on and on from there. For Clinton, however, the root of her problem with white men stems from a central aspect of benevolent sexism, according to Glick: its use as a tool to reward women who accept traditional gender roles, and punish those who don't. Any first lady who was discouraged from meddling in her husband's policy work, and received lavish praise for the food at a White House function, has first-hand experience of benevolent sexism.

And this is the crux of the gender issue for Clinton. An extensive body of research has shown that women who seek leadership positions often encounter resistance from both men and women if they violate gender norms by acting in stereotypically masculine ways, like being competitive, assertive and self-promotional.

[…]

"The more female politicians are seen as striving for power, the less they're trusted and the more moral outrage gets directed at them," said Terri Vescio, a psychology professor at Penn State who studies gender bias. "You're damned if you do and damned if you don't," she continued. "If you're perceived as competent, you're not perceived as warm. But if you're liked and trusted, you're not seen as competent."

[…]

This theoretical framework is extremely useful in decoding the real-life views of male voters like Tomi McKelvey, a 20-year-old beer store clerk who grew up in Dravosburg, a working-class town outside of Pittsburgh. McKelvey's father is a steel mill worker, and his mother is an accountant. He was an offensive lineman on his high school football team, and moves with the gracefulness of a former athlete. McKelvey, who is white, described himself as a moderate Republican. He disagrees with Trump's most inflammatory proposals, such as banning Muslim immigrants from entering the country. Still, he voted for Trump in the primary and is planning to back him again in the general election. He fits into

Trump's target demographic. If enough people like Tomi McKelvey vote for Trump, he has a real shot.

McKelvey told me he didn't like or trust Clinton. He said he wants a woman to become president someday, but didn't think that Clinton was the "right one."

"I'm not a real Hillary fan, but I respect her," McKelvey said.

When I asked him at another point if he viewed male and female roles in society any differently, McKelvey replied, "With a man you look for leadership and guidance. With a woman you look for companionship and nurturing. A motherly role."

McKelvey isn't unique in thinking this way. Many Americans have been conditioned to assign men and women prescribed gender roles. And when Clinton goes off-script, which she did a long time ago, and acts like a politician—that is to say, no different than a man—science shows that McKelvey and the rest of us are wired to judge her differently, and more negatively, than her male competition. That's the double standard at work, and that's the point. It is very real, and it has a profound effect on our view of men, women, and who gets to have the power.

[...]

In late May, I interviewed a group of five white men who get together each afternoon at the Mountaineer Cafe in Berlin, in southwestern Pennsylvania. The day we met at the diner, where a cup of coffee costs $1.55 and comes with a view of the main intersection in town, a light rain was falling outside. Don Williams, a 91-year-old retired welder, and Max Bowser, who is 75 and worked as a truck driver, were the first to arrive. They were soon joined by Elmer Altfather, 83, a retired carpenter; Ted Robb, 80, who worked for a railroad company; and Larry Pritts, 75, a retired heavy equipment operator and former member of Berlin's town council. The longtime friends are split along party lines: two are Democrats, and three are Republicans.

"Donald Trump scares me," Bowser, who is a Republican, said as our conversation got underway. "But we need a change, and I'm willing to give someone the right to change it."

Williams, who is also conservative, and has followed the election closely despite his advanced age, chimed in: "We need a big boom."

"Yeah," said Bowser. "But not Hillary. I don't like the way she lies. They've caught her in so many lies."

Bowser, like nearly every Republican voter I interviewed for this story, pointed to the Benghazi scandal, which took place on Clinton's watch as secretary of state and has haunted her political career ever since. House Republicans have spent years investigating the terrorist attacks, which killed four Americans in Benghazi, Libya in 2012, and grilled Clinton about her response to the incident in a memorable made-for-TV hearing last fall.

[...] One week before Clinton was slated to testify, Kevin McCarthy, the House majority leader, said on FOX News that the investigation was politically motivated. "Everybody thought Hillary Clinton was unbeatable, right? But we put together a special Benghazi committee," McCarthy said, and "what are her numbers today? Her numbers are dropping." At the hearing, Republicans struggled to provide evidence of a Clinton-led cover-up of the attacks, and Clinton appeared calm through nearly 11 hours of questioning. The press ruled that Republicans were the real "losers" and Clinton the real "winner." I covered the first several hours. At one point early on, Rep. Peter Roskam of Illinois was delivering a question from the dais when he noticed Clinton look down at a briefing book on the table in front of her. Cabinet members who testify before Congress routinely reference their notes during hearings, and are never called out for it. But Roskam stopped speaking and said, in an even tone that masked his condescension, "I can pause while you're reading your notes from your staff." Clinton looked up and answered, "I can do more than one thing at a time, congressman. Thanks."

In the diner, Bowser said that Benghazi stands for everything he finds wrong with Clinton. "There's a possibility I would vote for a woman. But not her," he added.

[...]

To some, the choice between a former first lady, senator and secretary of state and a real estate developer-turned-reality T.V. star will feel like a no-brainer. But for others it won't be that easy. They'll have doubts and fears, if they don't already. They'll be concerned about Clinton's policies, her personality, her email server and paid speeches on Wall Street. In the end, a certain percentage of white men aren't going to vote for Clinton in November, and if it's a large enough number Clinton is going to lose. And some of those men will not vote for Clinton simply because she's a woman, though they may not acknowledge that to pollsters or even themselves.

In the United Kingdom, Female Politicians Face Violence, Not Just Insults

Mona Lena Krook

In June 2016, Jo Cox, a member of the British Parliament, was shot and stabbed to death by a white supremacist shouting "Britain First!" during the nation's ugly fight over whether to leave the European Union. While male politicians have been assassinated (John Kennedy and Mohandas Gandhi, to name just two), women politicians are increasingly targeted with threats of violence. In the following viewpoint, Mona Lena Krook explores the consequences for democracy when women are threatened with violence when they serve their nations in political office. Krook is a professor of political science at Rutgers University in New Jersey.

As you read, consider the following questions:

1. Why are women politicians targeted more often and more violently than their male counterparts, according to this viewpoint?
2. How might bullying and harassment online and in political campaigns exacerbate the threat of in-person, physical violence?
3. How, according to the author, is this environment damaging for democracy?

"Democracy in Disarray When Violence Stalks Women MPs," by Mona Lena Krook, 2030 Foundation, 08/10/2017. http://www.broadagenda.com.au/home/rising-violence-against-women-in-politics/. Licensed under CC BY-ND 4.0 International.

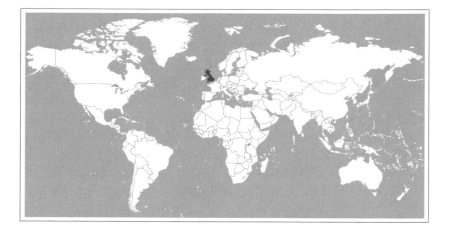

On 12 July, MPs took part in a Westminster Hall debate on abuse and intimidation of candidates and the public in the recent UK elections. During the debate, Chris Skidmore, the Minister for the Constitution, announced that Prime Minister Theresa May had requested that the Committee on Standards in Public Life carry out a review—firstly, to examine the nature of the problem and its implications for candidates and office holders and, secondly, to consider whether measures already in place to deal with this issue are sufficient, effective, and enforceable.

Research published in 2016 and 2017 indicates that the vast majority of British MPs have experienced "intrusive or aggressive behaviour" from constituents, while more than half of female MPs report having received physical threats. News reports suggest that intimidation and harassment have been on the rise for at least the last several years, with the online harassment of Stella Creasy being perhaps the most well-known case. The assassination of Jo Cox in June 2016, however, brought this issue into greater focus—and highlighted that women, in particular, appear to be targeted more often and more viciously than their male colleagues.

Although there were calls following Jo Cox's death for violent threats towards female MPs to be taken more seriously, incidents of online bullying and offline harassment seem—in contrast—to be growing more common. Over the past year, numerous MPs have reported online rape and death threats, including Jess Phillips, Yvette Cooper and Anna Soubry. In some cases, these attacks have occurred on multiple fronts, with misogyny combining with homophobia against Angela Eagle, racism against Diane Abbott, and anti-semitism against Luciana Berger.

Shortly after the 2017 general elections, some Conservative MPs began to share their experiences, with Sheryll Murray and Sarah Wollaston divulging threats received on social media, as well as incidents of vandalism and intimidation occurring at their homes and offices. In early July, the Citizens Commission on Islam, Participation, and Public Life published *Missing Muslims*, with a section detailing harassment of British Muslim women aspiring to participate in local politics.

Although these examples are rooted in the British context, they are not unique in a global perspective. The problem of violence and harassment against female politicians has been increasingly recognised by actors at the international, regional, and national levels.

In 2011, for example, the United Nations General Assembly approved Resolution 66/130, calling for zero tolerance for violence against female candidates and elected officials. In 2015, states-parties to the Inter-American Convention on the Prevention, Punishment, and Eradication of Violence against Women endorsed a Declaration on Political Harassment and Violence against Women. In 2017, the French Senate approved an amendment that would disqualify those found guilty of sexual or psychological harassment from holding political office.

In a recent article published in the *Journal of Democracy*, I map these emerging global debates, focusing on the nature of the problem, its implications for candidates and other office-holders, and solutions that might be employed by different actors to address this problem. These international experiences provide a useful starting point for the work of the Committee on Standards in Public Life, enabling it to focus its efforts on developing strategies to combat political violence and harassment in all its manifestations.

What Is Violence Against Women in Politics?

International actors typically define violence and harassment against women in politics as (1) aggressive acts toward female political actors, faced largely or only by women; (2) because they are women, often using gendered means of attack; (3) in order to deter their participation, as a way to preserve traditional gender roles and undermine democratic institutions.

This definition seeks to go beyond traditional understandings of political and electoral violence and harassment, understood as attempts to defeat or silence a particular political perspective through force. The democratic costs of such acts are often well-recognised.

Present debates seek to expand the discussion to address efforts to exclude and silence *women specifically*—sometimes due to their political affiliation, but also, more often, in spite of it. These forms of violence and harassment are largely obscured from public attention, either because they take place in private spaces or because, due to prevailing gender norms, they are widely naturalised and accepted.

The result is that female politicians often confront similar challenges as their male colleagues, stemming from their work as public servants, while *also* facing resistance and even danger in spaces accessible and safe for men—like political assemblies, party meetings, their offices, and their homes.

Differences in male and female politicians' experiences on social media illustrate these dynamics: while both women and men are (and, for democratic reasons, should be) criticised online for their policy positions, female MPs—and women who voice their opinions more generally—tend to be attacked in highly personalised, sexualised, and often vitriolic ways.

To be sure, there are high levels of political disaffection among the public towards politics and politicians and, when asked to compare the US Congress to a series of unpleasant things, respondents reported a higher opinion of root canals, cockroaches, and traffic jams.

Even in such a context, however, individuals tend to express greater levels of hostility toward female as compared to male leaders, judging women to be less likeable, qualified, and competent despite equivalent profiles. This antagonism stems from the fact that women are often seen as interlopers in the male world of politics, the result of a long history of silencing women's voices in the public sphere.

Devastating Consequences for Democracy

Normalising the abuse of public figures—and dismissing sexism and misogyny in the political world—as simply the "cost of doing politics" has devastating consequences for the quality of democracy.

First, it can undermine the will of voters by skewing electoral outcomes and rendering elected representatives less effective. Sexist comments and the sexual objectification of female politicians can have a critical impact on their electoral fortunes, while sexist hostility and intimidation can detract from substantive policy work and drive female politicians to step down.

Second, violence and harassment can impoverish political discourse by truncating the diversity of perspectives brought into the policy-making process. Women whose presence challenges multiple inequalities are frequently targeted, like Cécile Kyenge, the first black minister in Italy, who had bananas and racist epithets thrown at her.

Female politicians who speak and act from a feminist perspective are also attacked. Former Texas state senator Wendy Davis noted: "I have lots of bots who follow me. I could literally say it's a beautiful day in Texas and the responses I get on Twitter are 'baby murderer.'"

Third, violence and harassment directed at women can restrict women's political rights. Motivated by a desire to preserve traditional gender roles, perpetrators may target individual women, but in so doing, communicate a broader message that *women as a group* should not participate in politics.

This point is missed by free speech advocates who defend online trolling, overlooking the fact that the aim of such behaviour is to silence the targets, leading them to retreat from the public sphere. Young women have certainly internalised these lessons, dampening their own political ambitions.

In light of these consequences, unfortunately violence and harassment against female politicians is not rare. In a first attempt to measure this phenomenon, the Inter-Parliamentary Union interviewed female MPs across diverse countries in 2016 and found that more than 80% had experienced psychological abuse and more than 25% had confronted some form of physical violence.

Yet, to date, power dynamics between men and women in parliaments, parties, and society conspire to keep these behaviours hidden, treated as a regrettable but common occurrence in political life.

Fighting Perceptions That This Is Just "Politics As Usual"

Women's testimonies suggest that a wide range of perpetrators may be involved: while some abuse can be attributed to members of other political parties, a great deal also comes from women's own parties, their own communities, and their own families. Together with online harassers—whose identities are often more difficult to ascertain amid fake and anonymous accounts, as well as automated bots and communities of trolls—this landscape calls for a multi-level, multi-actor response.

A crucial first step is to resist dismissing violence and harassment as simply "politics as usual." In 2016, the National Democratic Institute (NDI) launched the #NotTheCost campaign to stop violence against women in politics, arguing that violence is *not* the cost of doing politics: women should be able to be politically active without experiencing discrimination, harassment, or assault.

At the state level, the National Commission on the Status of Women in Pakistan began collecting official data on violence against women in politics in 2015. In Mexico, various state agencies came together in 2016 to develop a protocol to coordinate their work to combat political violence and harassment.

Within parliaments, legislators have launched reforms to criminalise political violence and harassment, such as a law passed in Bolivia in 2012 and bills proposed in at least five other Latin American countries. In 2014, an all-party committee in the Canadian House of Commons instituted a new code of conduct and procedure for handling sexual harassment complaints.

Political parties have removed representatives, as the African National Congress in South Africa did in 2006, and considered barring members who perpetrate violence and harassment against other members or other parties, as recently proposed in France. Internally, the British Labour Party has instituted rules against sexism, racism, and bullying in party meetings. Liberal International made a statement on violence against women in politics before the UN Human Rights Council in 2016.

Technology companies, while crucial partners on the issue of online harassment, have not developed adequate policies for dealing with abuse against politicians—although Facebook has recently taken steps to tackle the spread of fake news stories. To date, users themselves have been the primary drivers of campaigns against online violence and harassment against women in politics through hashtags like #NotTheCost, #NameItChangeIt, and #ReclaimTheInternet.

These represent only a handful of potential solutions that have emerged to prevent and neutralise the damage caused by political violence and harassment.

There is no doubt, however, that global momentum is building as women and men around the world recognise that violence against women in politics poses a serious and growing threat to democracy. In the words of former US Secretary of State Madeleine Albright: "When a woman participates in politics, she should be putting her hopes and dreams for the future on the line, not her dignity and not her life."

In Latin America, the Media Encourages Sexist Portrayals of Women Leaders

Raiesa Frazer

In the following viewpoint, Raiesa Frazer points out that while many nations have elected female leaders—at many levels of government—sexist attitudes toward those leaders and the women they represent are still powerful. She goes on to examine several female leaders in Latin America to see how they are portrayed in the media, and in the end she concludes that if the world is to benefit from female leadership, it will have to change the way it presents women in power. Frazer is a research associate at the Council on Hemispheric Affairs.

As you read, consider the following questions:

1. How did the media react when Dilma Rousseff fell out of favor in Brazil? Would they have had a simliar reaction had she been a man?
2. Many of the negative portrayals of women leaders are not just sexist but sexual. Why do people take that particular approach to criticizing female politicians, according to the viewpoint?
3. After reading this viewpoint and the others in this chapter, how do you think attitudes in Latin America toward women politicians differ from those in the United States and Europe?

"Sexism in Politics 2016: What Can We Learn So Far from Media Portrayals of Hillary Clinton and Latin American Female Leaders?" by Raiesa Frazer, The Council on Hemispheric Affairs, June 16, 2016. Reprinted by permission.

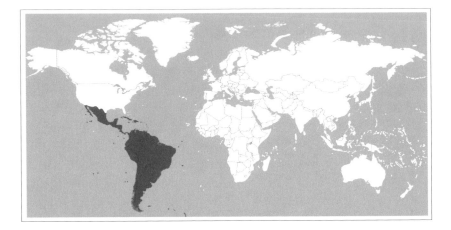

The history of sexism within the United States runs deep. While the United States seems to be ranked as one of the top nations in terms of its military, technology, and GDP, it still struggles with its social issues in terms of race, economic disparity, and gender inequality. After the efforts of the women's rights movement in the 1970's, women still seem to face discrimination in the workplace, on national television, or simply during their every day lives in regards to their gender. Today, women still struggle to express their ideas without being targeted for their sex or having it rejected by a male counterpart. The unity and support for women grew drastically in the United States with the breaking of societal, gendered barriers including appointing female CEO's, talented female athletes receiving high distinction, and most recently women entering combat. This year, the United States will face the strong possibility of electing a female candidate as President of the United States—a bold move that has already been achieved by many of its allies.

While the United States remains conflicted in electing a new female leader, countries in Latin America already have elected female presidents and are examining the legacies of such female leaders. Figures like Dilma Rousseff and Michelle Bachelet are recognized as the forerunners of guerrilla movements dedicated to ending the reign of military dictatorships in order to establish a democracy in their country. While female leaders in other

Latin American countries have not always taken part in political demonstrations, they have worked nearly twice as hard as their male counterparts in order to gain the positions they have today. According to *The Economist*'s "Wonder Women and Macho Men," women in Latin America are recorded as now spending more years in school than men, which suggests that their prospects and leadership skills will improve. Women have also climbed up the corporate ladder and became leaders within some of the world's largest energy companies, including Brazilian energy company Rede Energia and online retailer B2W.[1] Although the glass-shattering achievement of electing a woman into an executive office position has been achieved by multiple countries, there still remains discomfort in the general population of being able to trust a female leader. This includes women enacting legislation, handling foreign policy, and holding powerful public offices in the government. Based on the observations of the media's portrayal of Hillary Clinton's campaign, and of other high-profiled female presidents in the Americas, sexism has manifested itself through social media as an advanced form of expression and continues to be reinforced in society.

Hillary Clinton—the United States

Hillary Clinton has been the target of sexism since she launched her presidential campaign in 2016. Facing critiques on themes ranging from the tone of her voice to the outfits she wears to her interactions with her husband, Clinton has been constantly attacked on a personal level. Female critics argue that during the 2016 democratic debates, Clinton received questions that were much more difficult to respond to than those addressed to her male counterparts. In the Univision Democratic Debate on March 9, Clinton received questions from Jorge Ramos regarding deportation policies, her response to the attacks in Benghazi, Libya in 2012, and the handling of her email account. Since the Benghazi attack, Clinton has been the scapegoat for many politicians and analysts. Her interpretation of the situation was severely critiqued, and so was her sending of the video to her daughter. When forced to address whether she would drop out of the race if the Justice Department's investigation led to an indictment, she responded, "Oh for goodness—that's not going to happen. I'm not even going to answer that question."[2] Questions like these regarding the use of her personal email account and the possibility of being prematurely removed from the race may derive from deep societal misgivings towards having a woman running for an executive position. The intention of the questions was to appeal to Clinton's fears in order to shift her focus away from the presidency. Because none of the other male candidates had any executive office experience, she is critiqued on a different level than that of her other opponents. Her decision to respond to emails regarding Secretary of State information using her private email account should not be of such major concern for the elections. Many previous Secretaries of State, like John Kerry and Colin Powell, have also switched from using the Secretary of State email to using a personal email server that was under a firewall, too difficult to crack.[3] However, they have not been scrutinized severely by the public and office officials. Critiques of the candidate from daytime morning television shows and political talk shows have generated attention through the spread of social media comments. In a video created by *Huffington Post* tracking men's commentary on Clinton's vocal tone, male critics accuse her of "yelling" while suggesting that she should smile more during her speeches.[4] These critics even joke that Hillary will not receive male voters because of her tone being similar to men's "nagging wives" and reminiscent of the "lecture[s]" they receive from women in general.[5]

The clear undertone behind each of these comments were that the male critics were and are still challenged by Clinton's poise when giving speeches and taking part in Democratic debates. Her passion was misinterpreted as "yelling," while her serious demeanor was equated with strictness or anger. Although it is known for men to express this kind of anger, these male commentators expect Clinton to express her passion with a softer tone of voice, a common outlook that conflicts with women's own expectations in society today. This reveals how men in politics often are misguided in understanding sexism, leading their ignorance and own gender stereotype to emerge in the media or social networking sites. When such commentary generates outrage or backlash, they would be forced to address the issue since their career is put to the test but, at the same time, they would not understand that their commentary further continues the typical gender norms that society tries to break free from. While Clinton receives critiques for her campaign style, her counterparts, Bernie Sanders and Donald Trump, are also critiqued in terms of their platforms, responses to questions, and comments about their character by other presidential candidates. Only Sanders has rightfully agreed on the sexist comments made towards Clinton during election saying, "I can't think of many personalities who have been attacked for more reasons than Hillary Clinton. I don't know that a man would be treated the same way that Hillary is."[6] Donald Trump has also accused Hillary of playing the "Women's Card," a term used to assert that sexism against women is a tool used to exploit sexist attitudes, in a devaluing of her recent victories in several states.[7] While the "Women's Card" remains controversial in society, Trump takes his explanation a step further by appealing to male voters saying, "She's going— did you hear that Donald Trump raised his voice while speaking to a woman. Oh, I'm sorry. I'm sorry. I mean all of the men— we're petrified to speak to women anymore; we may raise our voice."[8] Trump seems to be using it to unite men against Clinton to warn that women are now more likely to become "aggressive" by "shouting" and not listen to what their male colleagues say. Of course, as popular culture has agreed through their use of the term "mansplaining," when a man raises his voice over a woman to get his point across, this is not the case.[9] Generally, women have been expressing their own opinions in politics. However, their male counterparts fail to adequately listen to their approach causing some men to raise their voices or reiterate their opinions in order to drown out their female counterparts. This clearly pushes the gendered stereotype that women must always agree with the man's point of view rather than having their own, a mindset that pushes society away from gender equality. As Clinton remains the likely Democratic Presidential nominee, it remains unclear if the United States is prepared to deal with a First Lady as its first female President.

Dilma Rousseff—Brazil

Dilma Rousseff, first female President of Brazil, remained popular during the first term of her presidency partially due to the economic prosperity left over from her predecessor's economic program *Bolsa Familia*, the exemption of federal tax of consumer basket products (essential food items), and the reduction of federal tax in the energy bill. However, during her second term, she failed to sustain the economy, allowing Brazil to enter one of its worst recessions, resulting in a very low popularity rating, falling below 10 percent. The Brazilian Supreme Court has also accused her of manipulating accounts through loans from the public banks that have enhanced the budget surplus and is currently awaiting trial. When the Chamber of Deputies, Brazil's lower house, voted in favor of continuing the impeachment process of Rousseff in the Senate, many of the officials in the overwhelmingly male chamber celebrated by holding premade posters with the slogan "*Tchau, querida!*" (Bye, love!). The phrase demonstrates their lack of respect for the president even though her allegations are not deemed as impeachable by those in favor of democracy in Brazil, as stated in a recent COHA report. As the proceedings continued, one of Brazil's magazines, *IstoÉ*, critiqued the female president as delusional, including false information claiming that she took prescription medication and swore thus labeling her as emotionally unstable.[10] As a result, several other magazine sources and activists picked up on the article's inappropriateness and attacked it for its blatant sexism and absurd references. Dilma is well aware of the sexism present in the criticisms she receives from the Chambers of Deputies, the Senate, and numerous political parties. In fact, she argues that the majority of the criticisms, including one that referred to her as "harsh," are a direct result of her gender.[11] Dilma's case is not the only example of sexism towards politicians in Brazilian media. Michel Temer's wife has also fallen victim to sexist comments in a *Veja* article headlined "Marcela Temer: bela, recatada, e 'do lar'" (Marcela Temer: Beautiful, Maiden like, and "A Housewife").[12] The tabloid paints the picture of Marcela Temer as a woman who has nothing else to offer besides the role of a typical household wife, which is clearly not true. While she and many Brazilian women do not specialize in politics, there are other achievements for which each woman is worth being recognized. When the Senate voted in favor of continuing with Dilma's impeachment trial, Vice President Temer assumed the executive post and filled his cabinet with white, wealthy, elite men, causing outrage among Brazil's diverse population.[13] This decision by the interim president caused Brazil to fall 22 points from position 85 to position 107 in the Global Index of Gender Inequality, a composite measure that captures the loss of achievement within a country due to gender inequality, making the country fall among the ranks of other developing countries including Brunei, Saudi Arabia, Pakistan, Hungary, and Slovakia.[14] In a country with so much diversity, Temer decided to adopt a homogeneous cabinet, a drastically different version of Dilma's cabinet. While the achievements of Dilma's party, the Workers Party, seem to have moved the country forward, the decisions Temer has set forth for the country adds to the sense that Brazil is moving backwards in time.

Cristina Fernandez de Kirchner, Michelle Bachelet, and Laura Chinchilla — Argentina, Chile, and Costa Rica

Despite her success in legalizing gay marriage, introducing a universal health care plan that boosted school attendance and reduced poverty, Kirchner still remained a target for the media as well as rival politicians who wished to see her take a more aggressive approach on Argentinian foreign policy. In 2012, *Noticia*, a tabloid news magazine, released an article entitled "Cristina's Pressure" and had a caricature of the Argentine president with "her head thrown back, her mouth open" making her seem as if she was "mid-orgasm" along with a slogan saying, "Every day she seems more confident, sensual and even shameless."[15] The media has been known to attack Kirchner on the basis of her looks rather than her accomplishments while in office. During her first election success, she was accused of being cold and distant, rather than being warm and open which she attempted to change the night after her re-election by inviting kids onto the stage to celebrate her win.[16] Once again, there is an application of societal feminine values reinforced on female officials. While it is inaccurate for her to be described as cold and distant, it shows how a male dominated mindset continues to interpret Kirchner and other female candidates as evil or emotionless instead of humble. Adding to the damage, Kirchner received nicknames from the wealthy class such as "Botox Evita" and "Bimbo."[17] She publicly acknowledged the fact that she loves to maintain her looks: "I've always got dressed up, caked on the make-up. Would I have to dress like I was poor in order to be a good political leader?"[18] Her honest statement highlights the scrutiny female politicians face based on their looks. In a society where perfection is key, especially in terms of physical features, women are ultimately pressured to conform to societal expectations of what a woman should look like and how she should act when representing the nation. While Kirchner remains a champion for the middle class and the poor, she is still dissected under the public eye based on her fiery speeches, her expression in her outfits, and her appeal to the larger global audience.

Michelle Bachelet took a progressive position by participating in guerilla groups dedicated to implementing democracy in a developing Chile. Since she became the first woman in office in 2014, many Chilean women have been more proactive in their societal demands. However, women are continuously reminded of Chile's societal chauvinism by media portrayals of Bachelet.

In the streets, local Chileans reference her as "*La Gordis*" ("the fat woman") and a magazine has labeled her as a "Baywatch babe" after finding a picture of her in a swimsuit.[19] The Finance Minister, Nicholas Eyzaguirre, even referenced her as "*mi gordi*" ("my fat woman") in an interview with *La Tercera* but later apologized, acknowledging the machismo undertones within his statement.[20] Within the political field, Bachelet's opponents fail to recognize her intentions as consensus-building and inclusive. Instead, they find her to be making "commissions" instead of "making decisions."[21] Many male politicians who are challenged by the authority of a woman continue to display immaturity and react unreasonably towards her progress in improving the country. So far, under her administration, her economic policies have helped the Chilean economy rebound from entering a recession. She provided social programs (i.e. "Chile Grows with You" in 2009), funded pension reforms, and developed a stimulus package to create jobs. While the stimulus package reduced poverty in the country, she also focused on improving childhood education through a program called, "I Choose my PC" in March 2009, where poor seventh graders with high achievement performance were rewarded free laptops to continue their learning. As a result of her efforts, she was appointed as first executive director of UN Women, a branch of the United Nations focusing on empowering women. Because of all these achievements, it seems understandable that Michele Bachelet would be the model that Chilean women seem to follow in order to continue change throughout their country. The biggest challenge Bachelet faces today is a corruption case against her family members and student protests as a result of her unkept promise to make universities free. Her future actions will determine whether or not she will continue to follow her proposed projects for the country and prove to contenders that she is still able to handle the presidency amidst all the pressure around her.

While the majority of the women in this analysis have pushed through controversial bills increasing the civil liberties of the LGBT community and women, several still hold onto the traditional values that were instilled in their country. For example, Costa Rica's first female president, Laura Chinchilla (2010–2014), has been praised for her handling of the border dispute between Costa Rica and Nicaragua, where she filed with the International Court of Justice against Nicaragua's decision to reclaim the Islands in the San Juan Delta, even though she had received mixed international criticism for her stances on abortion, same-sex marriage, and the separation of church and state. Women have evaluated her as someone who "doesn't really like women," or is "anti-woman" although this is not the case either.[22] Her focus has been on the economy (encouraged by biotechnology, organic agriculture, aerospace and aviation industries), and she also acknowledges the fact that she is representing the many women of Costa Rica and openly supports the progress of women by stating, "They say in a macho way that only men can lead. No way. We women can do it too."[23]

Conclusion

While a third of the world has already experienced an administration with a female in the executive position, the other two-thirds are challenged to meet that criteria and continue their efforts to eradicate the sexism that can be found within their local media and politics. Although this does not necessarily mean that one-third of the world is perfect, there should still be room for improvement on making sure women receive a strong representation in politics rather than one that mocks their credibility or undermines their knowledge. The source of sexism continues to be society reinforcing the pre-conceived roles women have been subjected to and forced within. As a result, once these pre-conceived thoughts are applied through the media, it continues to manifest, encouraging others to continue the degrading act which takes away from the real issues at hand. While one may be so quick to assume that men are the ones behind the sexism, it is actually both men and women who are equally to blame, revealing a disconnect in society's expectation to assess both genders equally. If society is serious about combating sexism, especially in politics, one step would be to define women in terms of the 21st century accomplishments they have made towards society's progress while encouraging other women to continue their lead in the future.[24]

Notes

1. "Wonder Women and Macho Men." *The Economist*. August 22, 2015. Accessed June 16, 2016. http://www.economist.com/news/americas/21661800-latin-american -women-are-making- great-strides-culture-not-keeping-up-wonder-women-and.

2. Laslo, Matt. "Democratic Debate: It's Painful to Watch Clinton and Sanders Go at Each Other | Matt Laslo." *The Guardian*. March 10, 2016. Accessed June 16, 2016. http:// www.theguardian.com/commentisfree/2016/mar/10/democratic-debate-painful -watch- clinton-sanders-go-at-each-other.

3. Parsons, Christi, and Michael A. Memoli. "Hillary Clinton's Use of Private Email Not Unusual, but Still Raises Questions." *Los Angeles Times*. March 03, 2015. Accessed June 16, 2016. http://www.latimes.com/nation/politics/politicsnow/la-pn-hillary -clinton-emails-20150303- story.html.

4. Wing, Nick. "Male Pundits To Hillary Clinton: Quiet Down And Smile More." *The Huffington Post*. March 15, 2016. Accessed May 09, 2016. http:// www.huffingtonpost.com/entry/male- pundits-hillary-clinton_us _56e8bc99e4b0860f99daecf6.

5. Ibid.

6. Hensch, Mark. "Sanders: Some Hillary Critics Are 'sexist'" *TheHill*. August 09, 2015. Accessed June 16, 2016. http://thehill.com/blogs/ballot-box/presidential -races/250677-sanders-some- hillary-critics-are-sexist.

7. Gearan, Anne, and Katie Zezima. "Trump's 'woman's Card' Comment Escalates the Campaign's Gender Wars." *Washington Post*. April 27, 2016. Accessed June 16, 2016. https://www.washingtonpost.com/politics/trumps-womans-card-comment -escalates-gender- wars-of-2016-campaign/2016/04/27/fbe4c67a-0c2b-11e6-8ab8 -9ad050f76d7d_story.html.

8. Khalid, Asma. "Is Donald Trump Playing The 'Man Card'?" NPR. May 10, 2016. Accessed June 16, 2016. http://www.npr.org/2016/05/10/477423028/is-donald -trump-playing-the-man-card.

9. *Merriam Webster*. "Mansplaining." *Merriam-Webster*. Accessed June 16, 2016. http:// www.merriam-webster.com/words-at-play/mansplaining-definition-history.

10. Pardellas, Sergio, and Débora Bergamasco. "Uma Presidente Fora De Si." *IstoÉ*. April 01, 2016. Accessed May 31, 2016. http://istoe.com.br/450027_UMA PRESIDENTE FORA DE SI/?pathImagens=&path=&actualArea=internalPage.

11. Shoichet, Catharine E. "Brazil's President: 'I Will Be Very Sad' If I Miss the Olympics." CNN. April 28, 2016. Accessed June 16, 2016. http://www.cnn.com/2016/04/27 /americas/brazil- president-dilma-rousseff-amanpour-interview/.

12. Sims, Shannon. "The Hilarious Feminist Backlash To Brazil's Impeachment Fallout." *Forbes*. April 20, 2016. Accessed June 16, 2016. http://www.forbes.com /sites/shannonsims/2016/04/20/the-hilarious- feminist-backlash-to-brazils -impeachment-fallout/?ss=leadership-leaders#3359c5ad59fa.

13. Sims, Shannon. "Brazil's New President Michel Temer Fills Cabinet With Only White Men." *Forbes*. May 12, 2016. Accessed June 16, 2016. http://www.forbes.com/sites

/shannonsims/2016/05/12/brazils- new-president-michel-temer-fills-cabinet
-with-only-men/#693f423c40c6.

14. Wentzel, Marina. "Sem Ministras, Brasil Perde 22 Posições Em Ranking De Igualdade
De Gênero." BBC Brasil. May 25, 2016. Accessed June 16, 2016. http://www.bbc
.com/portuguese/brasil- 36355724?ocid=socialflow_facebook.

15. "Wonder Women and Macho Men." *The Economist*. August 22, 2015. Accessed June
16, 2016. http://www.economist.com/news/americas/21661800-latin-american
-women-are-making-great-strides- culture-not-keeping-up-wonder-women-and.

16. D.R. "Wonder Women and Macho Men." *The Economist*. October 24, 2011. Accessed
June 16, 2016. http://www.economist.com/news/americas/21661800-latin
-american-women-are-making-great-strides- culture-not-keeping-up-wonder
-women-and.

17. Goni, Uki. "Cristina Kirchner: She's Not Just Another Evita | Profile." *The Guardian*.
February 04, 2012. Accessed June 16, 2016. http://www.theguardian.com
/theobserver/2012/feb/05/observer-profile- cristina-kirchner-argentina.

18. Thomas White International. "Global Players." Thomaswhite.com. August 2009.
Accessed May 27, 2016. http://www.thomaswhite.com/global-perspectives
/cristina-fernandez-de-kirchner-president- argentina/.

19. Balch, Oliver. "Michelle Bachelet: The Cultural Legacy of Chile's First Female
President." *The Guardian*. December 13, 2009. Accessed June 16, 2016. http://
www.theguardian.com/world/2009/dec/13/michelle-bachelet-chile-president
-legacy.

20. Emol. "Eyzaguirre Le Pide Disculpas a Bachelet Por Llamarla 'mi Gordi.'" Emol.
August 22, 2005. Accessed June 16, 2016. http://www.emol.com/noticias
/nacional/2005/08/22/192982/eyzaguirre-le- pide-disculpas-a-bachelet-por
-llamarla-mi-gordi.html.

21. Ibid.

22. Samhita. "Feministing." Feministing. Accessed June 16, 2016. http://feministing
.com/2010/02/12/laura-chinchilla-first-female-president-of-costa-rica-doesnt
-really-like-women/.

23. *Global Post*. "Costa Rica: A Woman in Charge?" *GlobalPost*. May 04, 2010. Accessed
June 16, 2016. http://www.globalpost.com/dispatch/costa-rica/100204/laura
-chinchilla-elections.

24. Greve, Joan E. "Study: 'Entitled' Men and Women Are More Sexist." *Time*. June 06,
2014. Accessed June 16, 2016. http://time.com/2839352/study-entitled-men-and
-women-are-more-sexist/.

Periodical and Internet Sources Bibliography

The following articles have been selected to supplement the diverse views presented in this chapter.

Christina Asquith, "This Week in Women: The Fight Against Sexism in Politics Worldwide Goes On," *Ms.*, June 8, 2018. http:// msmagazine.com/blog/2018/06/08/week-women-fight-sexism -politics-worldwide-goes.

Erin Cassese, Tiffany D. Barnes, and Mirya Holman, "How 'Hostile Sexism" Came to Shape Our Politics," *Washington Post*, October 2, 2018. https://www.washingtonpost.com/news/monkey-cage /wp/2018/10/02/who-supports-kavanaugh-after-last -weeks-angry-hearings-our-research-helps-explain/?utm _term=.092d46afe281.

Josie Cox, "Angela Merkel Is the World's Most Powerful Woman— So She'd Better Start Calling Herself a Feminist," *Independent*, September 19, 2017. https://www.independent.co.uk/voices /angela-merkel-chancellor-germany-powerful-feminism-gender -roles-a7955526.html.

Faras Ghani, "Shin Ji-ye and Her Aim to Challenge Sexism in Korean Politics," Al Jazeera, September 21, 2018. https://www.aljazeera .com/news/2018/09/shin-ji-ye-aim-challenge-sexism-korean -politics-180911091915414.html.

Joshua Holland, "Trump Has Made Republicans More Comfortable Expressing Their Sexism Out Loud," *Nation*, October 12, 2018. https://www.thenation.com/article/trump-has-made -republicans-more-comfortable-expressing-their-sexism-out -loud.

Kate Lyons, "Majority of Men in Middle East Survey Believe a Woman's Place Is in the Home," *Guardian*, May 2, 2017. https:// www.theguardian.com/global-development/2017/may/02 /majority-of-men-in-middle-east-north-africa-survey-believe -a-womans-place-is-in-the-home.

Emma Newburger, "Female Candidates Are Calling Out Sexism More Aggressively on the Campaign Trail," CNBC, September 27, 2018. https://www.cnbc.com/2018/09/27/female-candidates-are-more-aggressive-about-tackling-gender-based-attacks-in-2018-election.html.

Nancy Okail, "Policy Experts Decry Middle East Sexism. What About Sexism in Our Own Profession?," *Washington Post,* August 16, 2016. https://www.washingtonpost.com/posteverything/wp/2016/08/16/policy-experts-decry-middle-east-sexism-what-about-sexism-in-our-own-profession/?utm_term=.d13eb413195a.

Rick Rojas, "Women in Australia's Parliament Denounce Sexism in a Push for Change," *New York Times*, September 10, 2018. https://www.nytimes.com/2018/09/10/world/australia/women-parliament-sexism-bullying.html.

Stéphanie Thomas, "Three Times Women Shut Down Sexism in Politics," World Economic Forum, May 19, 2016. https://www.weforum.org/agenda/2016/05/we-won-t-stay-quiet-anymore-3-times-women-shut-down-sexism-in-politics.

Jessica Valenti, "Trump Did to Merkel What Men Do to Women All the Time," *Guardian*, March 21, 2017. https://www.theguardian.com/commentisfree/2017/mar/21/trump-did-to-merkel-what-men-do-to-women-all-the-time.

GLOBALVIEWPOINTS

| Looking Ahead

In the United Kingdom, Quotas Are Needed to Get Women into Politics

Alexandra Topping and Jessica Elgot

In the following viewpoint, Alexandra Topping and Jessica Elgot describe a Women in the World event in London in 2015. Many women—heads of state, lawyers, activists, scientists, and even celebrities—weighed in on ways to promote gender equality in politics. Nicola Sturgeon, first minister of Scotland, directly addressed the need for quotas. Others discussed issues such as domestic violence, trolling of female leaders, post-feminism, and backlash when women do make progress. Topping is a news reporter for the Guardian. *Elgot is a political correspondent for the* Guardian.

As you read, consider the following questions:

1. According to the viewpoint, what did Theresa May say kept women from getting involved in politics?
2. How did Nicola Sturgeon link domestic violence and gender inequality?
3. Why might considering domestic violence calls vexatious be a serious problem for women and society at large?

Two of the UK's most powerful women in government have been challenged on the political gender gap at a conference, with the home secretary Theresa May suggesting that women could be turned off from politics because of the aggressive "rough and

"Quotas Needed to Help Women Enter Politics, Says Nicola Sturgeon," Guardian News and Media Limited, October 9, 2015. Reprinted by permission.

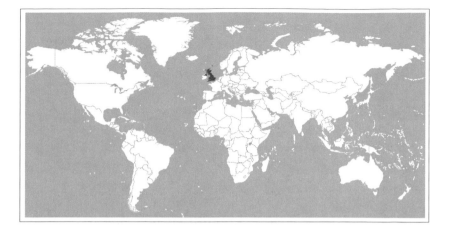

tumble," while Scotland's first minister, Nicola Sturgeon, said she favoured a quota system to help females.

As women's rights and gender equality were put centre stage at the Women in the World event in London on Friday, May said she did not believe the difficulty in balancing work and family life was discouraging women from becoming MPs. But she suggested that the most visible parts of politics, such as the adversarial prime minister's questions, could put women off.

"Women will look at the most-seen part of politics, which is the rough and tumble, and think they can can apply their talents elsewhere," she said. But she said being a woman had not held her back. "Every time I tried to do something, I tried never to think that if it failed it was because I was a woman. I tried to think: what questions didn't I answer?"

Sturgeon applauded the Sisters Uncut protest at the red carpet opening of the film *Suffragette*, which was prompted by government cuts to domestic violence services. "Domestic violence is a symbol of gender inequality, but is also a cause of gender inequality," she said, highlighting current moves by the Scottish parliament to make domestic violence an aggravating factor in sentencing.

In a tense exchange with interviewer Sir Harold Evans, where he said police had to be cautious in case domestic violence calls were "vexatious," Sturgeon said: "I don't think any call from a

Here's How to Make Quotas Work

Moldova has recently adopted a 40 percent quota for the least represented gender in governmental offices and on the electoral lists for local and parliamentary elections. But according to our data, this has not led to the expected increase in representation for women.

Quotas for women and men in decision-making positions are one of the most common ways of ensuring that women don't have to face the glass ceiling when advancing in the ranks of political parties and that they have equal chances to be represented in governments and legislatures.

However, sometimes the provisions of quota legislation can be too weak to have an impact.

In Moldova, the recently adopted law does not make any specifications about the placement of women and men in the candidate lists. This omission may seem innocuous, but the reality is that women often find themselves relegated to the bottom of lists, with only one in five candidates at the top being a woman.

We believe that things can only be changed if the problem is acknowledged. To reach that point, three things must happen:

1. The electoral authority must acknowledge the problem and be cooperative in finding ways to fix it;

2. A complete electoral database must be set up to allow for continuous in-depth analysis of data and trends that could be used to redesign public policies and bridge gender gaps; and

3. Partnerships need to be established between the government, civil society, and international organizations like UNDP and UN Women to support the advancement of women in political and public life.

Only then will we be able to say we are moving towards a more equal world for women and men.

"We Need More Women in Politics—Here's How to Make Quotas Work," United Nations Development Programme, July 11, 2016.

woman reporting abuse should be treated as vexatious. We are seeing the rate of prosecution go up very sharply. There's a massive effort going into this and that is right and proper. We need to drive forward gender equality, but we won't do that if women are held back by violence and abuse."

Sturgeon said she believed quotas in politics were necessary to speed up the pace of change. "I don't want my nine-year-old niece to still be fighting these battles," she said. "I don't believe it is good for any of us to underuse the talents of 50% of the population."

After May said she felt women often needed a "tap on the shoulder" before they felt confident enough to go into politics, the SNP's Mhairi Black said she had previously had no political ambitions. "There was real momentum after the referendum," the 21-year-old MP said, revealing she had been so relaxed on the day of the election that she stayed away from the count, watching *The Big Bang Theory* on TV at home.

"I had to stand because there was no one else willing to do it. They guilt-tripped me into putting myself forward," she said.

Westminster was desperately lacking diversity—in gender, background and ethnicity, Black said. "Otherwise it becomes a stale, middle-class, middle-income boys' club. That's what Westminster is—it still has that boys' club feeling to it. It's alive and well in Westminster."

The need for dramatic action was clear, said Catherine Mayer of the Women's Equality party, pointing out that there are currently more male MPs than the historical total of female parliamentarians. There are also, she added, "more men named John leading FTSE 100 countries in the UK than there are women."

Defending the need for a single issue party, she said the pace of change had been so slow as to be glacial. "The one language political parties understand is the power of the ballot box."

The star-studded two-day event was organised by Tina Brown, former editor of the *New Yorker*, and started with a standing ovation for women from the Ford car plant in Essex whose battle for equal pay in the late 60s was immortalised in the 2010 film *Made in Dagenham*.

The event concluded with the first interview with Tor Pekai Yousafzai, the mother of Nobel prize winning girls' rights campaigner, Malala Yousafzai.

The opening night on Thursday saw actor Meryl Streep urging women not to give up the fight for equal rights. It also featured Germany's first female defence minster, Ursula von der Leyen, a mother of seven who as labour minster introduced shared parental leave in Germany, calling for men to join the struggle. She said: "If you fight for women's rights, you need modern men as your allies."

There were calls for women to be more "disobedient," with author Kathy Lette saying that any woman describing herself as a post-feminist had "kept her Wonderbra and burned her brains."

The audience also heard from barrister Charlotte Proudman, who became the focus of a worldwide media frenzy after she spoke out about a sexist message she had received on social networking service LinkedIn. She said trolling was a way to stop women speaking out. "The backlash was something I never expected. I had death threats, threats to separate my head from my body. I was called a bitch and a ball-busting munter. It is still going on. And it is simply because I challenged vested male interests and that is something I refuse to apologise for."

Nicole Kidman, who is currently playing Rosalind Franklin—a key member of the team that discovered DNA's helix structure—in the West End play *Photograph 51*, also spoke. She revealed that the night she won an Oscar for *The Hours* in 2003 was the "loneliest I have ever felt."

Speaking candidly about her emotional state after her divorce from the actor Tom Cruise, she said: "To be completely honest, I was running away from my life. I couldn't handle the reality of my life. Out of that came work that was applauded and that was interesting for me."

She said she believed there was "absolutely" still a shortage of great female roles on stage and screen, but it could not simply be a matter of rewriting male characters for women. "Let's tell the female stories too. Let's tell the story of Rosalind Franklin, of the suffragettes—there are so many extraordinary stories to be told."

In a panel discussion about selfies and low self-confidence, psychologist Susie Orbach said body dislike was "stealing the childhood" of girls, who were "learning about display as the way to interact with the world rather than contribution." She warned that multinational companies were preying on the insecurities of a generation that "has to be a brand that we sell."

"It's not just affecting girls, but boys," she said. "If you can get as many boys to hate themselves as girls, there is a lot of money to be made."

From the world of science, Dr Margaret Aderin-Pocock—who joked that there were now fewer dinosaurs expressing disbelief that a black woman could also be a scientist—urged women to throw themselves into the limelight. "There are opportunities out there, but if we don't take them, then we waste them," she said.

VIEWPOINT

In Spain, a Majority-Female Cabinet Bodes Well for the Future of Gender-Equal Governments Around the World

Susan Franceschet and Karen Beckwith

In the following viewpoint, Susan Franceschet and Karen Beckwith describe what they call "the concrete floor" for women's political representation. This is the fact that when women reach the highest levels of government leadership, their numbers in government tend to rise. The authors explain that when male leaders appoint women to high-level cabinet and minister positions, these men are rewarded at the polls. Franceschet is a professor of political science at the University of Calgary. Beckwith is a professor of political science at Case Western Reserve University.

As you read, consider the following questions:

1. As of this writing, what country had the highest number of female cabinet officers?
2. According to the authors, how does appointing women to these positions help boost the number of other women in government?
3. What balances, other than gender, in cabinet representation are mentioned by the authors?

"What Spain's Majority-Female Cabinet Says About the Future of Gender-Equal Governments," World Economic Forum, July 17, 2018. Reprinted by permission.

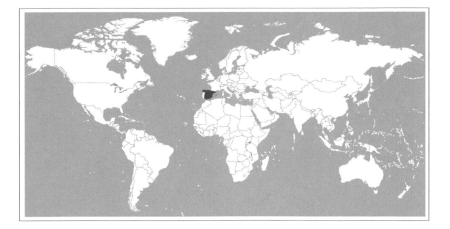

G ender-equal governments, which include the same number of men and women as ministry heads and in other cabinet posts, used to be the purview of woman-friendly Nordic countries and highly progressive societies like Canada and Costa Rica.

No longer.

Mexico's president-elect Andrés Manuel López Obrador, who takes office in December, has announced that women will hold eight posts in his 16-member cabinet, including the powerful secretary of the interior position.

And Spain's new prime minister, Pedro Sánchez, recently became the first world leader to appoint women to almost two-thirds of cabinet positions. No country in the world has a higher proportion of female-led ministries. Thirty years ago, Spain had no female cabinet members.

Women hold just 20 per cent of cabinet positions in the United States and 28 percent in the United Kingdom. Worldwide, the average is 18.3 percent.

As political scientists who study women's inclusion in cabinets, we believe the quick, steady rise of women to power in Spain embodies a trend we have observed worldwide: Once more women get into the highest levels of government, their numbers tend only to rise.

We call this the "concrete floor" for women's political representation. For a democratic government to have legitimacy these days—that is, for the general public to have faith in its decisions—it must include women.

Gains Beget Gains

Women's representation doesn't necessarily go up with each new administration.

But in studying the composition of governing cabinets in Spain, France, Australia, the United States, Canada, Chile and the United Kingdom from 1929 to 2016, we found that women's presence did rise cumulatively—over time and across party lines—in these countries.

After a 40-year dictatorship led by General Francisco Franco, democracy returned to Spain in 1977. But it would take more than a decade for women to be included in government. Socialist Prime Minister Felipe González appointed the country's first female ministers in 1989.

The next administration, led by conservative prime minister José María Aznar, raised the total with four female ministers in his 14-member cabinet.

Spain's historic breakthrough came in 2004, when Socialist Prime Minister José Luis Rodríguez Zapatero, a self-described feminist, named the country's first gender-equal cabinet: eight women and eight men.

Now 11 of Spain's 17 ministers are women, including—for the first time in Spain's history—the position of finance minister.

France's recent history looks similar.

President Nicolas Sarkozy appointed seven women to his 15-member cabinet in 2007. His successor, Socialist François Hollande, had 17 women in his 34-member cabinet. Cabinet size in most countries varies from administration to administration.

On the campaign trail in 2016, President Emmanuel Macron promised to have equal representation. Today, his cabinet contains 11 women and 11 men.

Voters Like Gender-Inclusive Governments

Our research shows that when leaders use their powers of appointment to increase the number of women in cabinet, they are never punished electorally and are often applauded globally for doing so.

Just a few years ago Canadian Prime Minister Justin Trudeau was celebrated around the world for assembling a gender-equal cabinet. His reasoning? "Because it's 2015," he told reporters.

Leaders who appoint significantly fewer women than their predecessors, on the other hand, risk heavy criticism from the media and political opponents. That can weaken their support among voters.

When Australian prime minister Tony Abbott appointed just one woman to his cabinet in 2013, he had to justify his "embarassing" decision to voters, the opposition party and the press. His predecessor's government had included three female cabinet members.

Malcolm Turnbull replaced Abbott two years later and quickly appointed five women to his governing team.

Each gender-equal cabinet appears to create expectations of similar or greater women's inclusion in the next.

The "Concrete Floor"

We did find several instances where leaders appointed fewer women than their predecessors. However, the decline is generally minimal.

In Chile's first post-dictatorship government, elected in 1990, President Patricio Aylwin apointed women to just 5 percent of cabinet posts.

Chile's first female president, Socialist Michelle Bachelet, had a gender-equal government in 2006. Four years later, her conservative successor, Sebastián Piñera, appointed seven women to his 23-member cabinet. While his government was not gender-equal, women were significantly better represented than they had been before Bachelet's administration.

We call this phenomenon the "concrete floor." It is the minimal threshold of women's inclusion for people to see a leader's cabinet as democratically legitimate.

And unlike the "glass ceiling," that subtle, invisible barrier that has kept women out of powerful positions, the concrete floor ensuring their inclusion in government is visible to—and recognized by—all the leaders we studied.

Gender Diversity Is the Only Guarantee

A similar standard applies to certain other kinds of political representation in some, but not all, of the countries we studied.

In Canada, Germany and Spain, for example, cabinets must be geographically representative. Like those countries, the United States also has a federal system of government, but American presidents are not expected to ensure that cabinet posts go to people from different states or regions.

In Canada and the United States, all-white cabinets are now virtually unthinkable. President Lyndon Johnson appointed United States' first African-American cabinet member—Secretary of Housing and Urban Development Robert C. Weaver—in 1966. Lincoln McCauley Alexander became Canada's first-ever black minister in 1979.

Meanwhile, cabinets in Germany and Spain—both increasingly diverse countries—remain entirely white. The lone black parliamentarian in Spain, Rita Bosaho, wasn't elected until 2015. No racial minority has ever held a Spanish cabinet position.

Gender was the only required representational criterion that appeared across all seven countries we studied, where all-male cabinets have been universally extinct for a quarter-century.

Women make up half the world's population. Now, increasingly and evidently irreversibly, democratic governments are starting to show it.

Democracy Requires That Women Take Part in Making Laws

Michelle Bachelet

In the following viewpoint, in an address given at the Democracy and Gender Equality Roundtable in May 2011, Michelle Bachelet stresses that women need to participate in government in order to advance gender equality. At the time of the roundtable, Bachelet was under-secretary-general and executive director of UN Women. Bachelet was the first woman to be elected president of Chile. She served in that position from 2006 to 2010 and again from 2016 to 2018. Bachelet argues that women are playing an active role in pro-democracy protests and in how the world's concept of democracy is changing to include participation by all people, not just landowning males.

As you read, consider the following questions:

1. According to the viewpoint, what is necessary for women to achieve complete equality?
2. How does Bachelet describe the slogan "the personal is political"?
3. Bachelet says that women's voices are necessary for accountability. How is this so, according to her remarks?

"Democracy and Gender Equality," UN Women, May 5, 2011. Reprinted by permission.

L adies and Gentlemen,
        This year may well mark the beginning of the "fourth wave" of democracy. As we have seen from the dramatic events of the "Arab spring," women have been actively involved in the new wave of demands for political freedoms and dignity. In the streets of Tunis and Cairo and more recently in Sanaa, it has been difficult not to notice that women from all walks of life have joined the ranks of protestors in the streets to raise their voices for democracy and citizenship. As a result, we are already beginning to see gains for some women.

In April of this year, the political reformers of Tunisia achieved what had been unthinkable only months earlier; a draft electoral law calling for full parity in the political representation of the new Tunisian democracy. The law proposes that in the next parliamentary elections candidate lists will alternate between women's and men's names.

These events remind us of how fundamentally democracy has changed since its inception. Once considered to be the sole domain of landowning male elites, it is now impossible to think of democracy as anything but full and equal political citizenship for all. Of course this must be driven by leadership and commitment at the highest levels to ensure women's full and equal participation in democratic processes.

This morning I will focus on what we have learned from women's participation in democratic decision-making; that is, three key elements that must guide democracy assistance.

First, we need to address the obstacles women face in participation in the electoral process and their ability to exercise a real choice in elections. Second, we must consider whether spaces are created for women to articulate policy preferences or voice. Third, democratic public institutions must be accountable to women.

First allow me to start with the issues of choice. Over time democracy, as a political system, has developed mechanisms to integrate marginalized groups mechanisms such as quotas or regional arrangements to amplify the concerns of politically disenfranchised groups. Women are often in the majority of populations, yet they face a wide range of constraints to effective participation even in the most basic of democratic exercises, such as voting, or running for political office. Ironically, even in 2011 we do not have accurate data on the numbers of women compared to men who register to vote in many countries, or who actually exercise the vote. We have even less data on the extent to which women's independent choice is constrained by coercion within the household or practical problems like a lack of mobility or violence at the polls.

The consequences of constraints on participation are well-known. Women make up less than 20% of legislators and less than 5% of ministers. Women have found themselves consistently constrained by traditional gender roles in the exercise of their political rights even in the most robust of democracies.

The second constraint regards effective voice. Effective public participation depends on being able to articulate interests and form a constituency to advance those interests. We have to ask ourselves—do we put enough resources into women's civil society organizations so that women can pursue their interests? Do political parties reflect and respond to women's concerns? We must remember that democracies can deliver majorities that actually—in the name of a democratic process—can impose restrictions on women's rights. This can happen when there is not enough diversity and voice for women in politics.

If political party and government structures do not take into account women's needs and priorities, and the media and traditional and cultural practices consistently minimize women's value in political life, then democracies cannot deliver for women. What is more, the quality of democracy itself is weakened. Susan B Anthony, a famous campaigner for women's right to vote, said "There never will be complete equality until women themselves help to make laws and elect lawmakers."

And finally, we have to ask whether democratic institutions answer to women. True democracy is about more than just participation—it is about the checks and balances and accountability institutions that allow women to seek redress when their rights are abused and their needs are ignored.

The judiciary, parliamentary oversight processes, and public audit institutions, all need to ensure that their procedures and standards are designed to monitor women's rights violations and to enable women to call for inquiries and reviews. If these institutions are not in place and functioning, it sends a message to women that their citizenship rights are weaker than those of men, and indeed that their rights to security, to fair pay, or to property are subordinated to men's rights. If women cannot hold government accountable for promoting gender equality then women's citizenship is on fragile foundations.

Many of you here will remember the slogan of the 1970s: "the personal is political." This slogan reflected the fact that inequality in the private sphere undermines equality in the public sphere. Public laws and institutions can reinforce those private inequalities. This can prevent institutions from truly answering to women. There is another women's slogan that came from my own country during our democratic transition: "democracy at home and in the state." The logic is the same; a democratic state should be held accountable for abuses of women's rights. Full and true participation is not possible unless there is equality in everyday life. This extends not only to gender equality but to the need to address vast economic disparities as well—which pose extremely serious threats to democracy.

UN Women's programming addresses these issues of choice, voice, and accountability. Around the world UN Women has supported women's movements' efforts to get women to vote and to run for political office, supporting training for candidates and working with media to generate better quality reporting on women's campaigns.

In Tunisia and Egypt, UN Women is supporting women in civil society to identify their priorities for constitutional reform.

In Egypt, the Democratic Republic of Congo, and in many other contexts, UN Women has supported country consultations between women's civil society organizations and political leaders in order to develop Women's Charters. These Charters list women's priorities for a gender responsive democracy, such as electoral gender quotas, consultations between gender equality constituencies and politicians, and building networks of elected women parliamentary caucuses, among others.

UN Women also supports initiatives to strengthen gender accountability in the public administration through gender-responsive budgeting and with programmes in Rwanda and Tajikistan that develop a feedback loop between public service providers and women citizens. UN Women has worked with the office of the High Commission on Human Rights to support countries to address violations of women's rights through support to Commissions of Inquiry and truth and reconciliation commissions. UN Women also supports countries around the world to put in place national legislative commitments to international policy and legal instruments such as the Beijing Platform for Action, the Convention on the Elimination of All Forms of Discrimination Against Women, the Africa Union protocol on the Rights of Women, and the Southern African Development Community protocol on gender.

To summarize, three basic requirements are critical for making democracy real for women. First, we have to remove the obstacles that keep women from participating effectively: mobility, finances, access to information, lack of public safety, and coercion, intimidation and violence.

Second, we must recognize that participation is one thing but real voice is another. Are women able to articulate and voice their rights, needs and preferences? How far are political parties internally democratic? Have women in civil society had the opportunity to debate common positions on the constitution, electoral law, safety during campaigns, and other issues?

Third and finally, democratic institutions have to be held accountable to women, and held accountable for meeting commitments to women's rights.

If a democracy neglects women's participation, if it ignores women's voices, if it shirks accountability for women's rights, it is a democracy for only half its citizens.

I look forward to hearing the recommendations that come from the discussions today so that we can enhance our democracy assistance. I recognize in the list of speakers and this audience today, many important democracy activists. We are privileged that you are participating today. The great courage shown by women and men across the world in this dawning of a potential fourth wave of democracy calls on every one of us to make sure that gender equality is addressed in our efforts to make democracy real for all.

In Europe, Gender Equality Is Necessary for Modern Democracy to Survive

European Women's Lobby

In the following viewpoint, the European Women's Lobby discusses the seminar entitled "My MEP [member of the European Parliament] is just like me." The meeting was organized to discuss issues surrounding women's representation in European government. The report covers many issues and positions taken by the speakers, including one who noted that the European Parliament is not truly representative of its members, not only because it doesn't have enough women, but because it is lacking in LGBT members and ethnic diversity as well. Other panelists discussed ways to rectify this situation. The European Women's Lobby advocates for women's human rights and equality between women and men.

As you read, consider the following questions:

1. What percentage of Parliament was made up of women at the time of the meeting?
2. How does this viewpoint suggest that racism and gender discrimination are intertwined?
3. What advice did the US congresswoman have to offer the European delegates to this seminar?

"'No Modern European Democracy Without Gender Equality': Unity in Diversity," Womenlobby.org, March 12, 2014. Reprinted by permission.

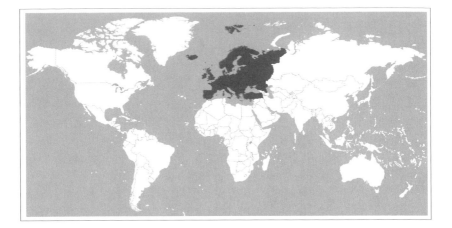

O n 18 February, the European Women's Lobby organised a seminar on gender equality and diversity in European Political Life. The seminar "My MEP is just like me?!" was hosted by MEP Claude Moraes (S & D) at the European Parliament in Brussels and was organised within the framework of the EWL 50/50 Campaign for parity democracy in the European Institutions and at national level, and for the integration of gender equality as a priority in all policies. Among others, MEPs of the 50/50 campaign's Core GroupUlrike Lunacek (Green), Zita Gurmai (S & D) and Sirpa Pietikänen (EPP), Antoniya Parvanova (ALDE) and Claudette Abela Baldacchino (S & D) supported the event and moderated the discussions of the three panels and over a hundred participants.

Claude Moraes MEP (S & D)

In his opening speech MEP Claude Moraes pointed out that the current European Parliament is not really representative of the diversity of people in Europe because less than 2% of its Members are from an ethnic minority, and only 35% of its Members are women. In order to address this under-representation, he proposed that, during their meetings, political groups put gender equality and anti-discrimination higher up on their agenda. He also expressed his strong support for the EWL political mentoring programme as a concrete measure to ensure that there is parity and diversity in the next European Parliament.

MEP Ulrike Lunacek moderated the first panel which focused on framing the current situation of women, including from minority groups such as LGBTI, in political life, and on highlighting a series of success factors.

Petra Meier, Assistant Professor in Politics at the University of Antwerp

Petra Meier presented some facts and figures on the evolution of women in politics over the last three decades in Europe, while identifying discrepancies of representation rates between different Member States. The Assistant Professor in Politics at the University of Antwerp considers that it is an achievement for women to have succeeded in keeping the issue of parity on the agenda, particularly because of the persistent obstacles that prevent women from participating in political life. She mentioned more specifically structural obstacles (e.g. party and political systems) and cultural thresholds (e.g. rituals, practices and symbols), and pointed to the relative short stay of women in politics, the lack of diversity and the absence of data, as issues that needed to be addressed by political parties in the near future. In relation to diversity, she stressed that being a lesbian, bisexual, or transgender politician was still not acceptable in the political sphere. Assistant Professor Meier concluded by indicating that, although it was important to have parity and diversity in politics, she called for vigilance to avoid the instrumentalisation of diversity, and particularly that of women from ethnic minorities, by political parties and politicians.

Congresswoman Linda Sánchez, Senior Whip for the Democratic Caucus, USA

"If you don't have a seat at the table, chances are that you are on the menu." In her speech, Congresswoman Sánchez, who traveled from Los Angeles to speak at the seminar, reminded the audience that it is indeed possible for women from diverse backgrounds to develop a successful career in politics. She mentioned the necessity to have role models in politics as paramount for women to engage in political life in the first place. As an example, she explained how her decision to go into politics was inspired by her sister's election to office and her parents' courageous journey as migrants from Mexico. However, Congresswoman Sánchez deplored the underrepresentation of women and particularly women from minorities in American political life. For example, in the US Congress 16% of members are women (only 9 of these women are Latinas). Moreover, voters are less likely to cast their vote and less likely to go into politics in the absence of politicians whom they can identify with.

In this sense, she called for parity and more women who are ethnically diverse in US politics. As a possible solution, Congresswoman Sánchez proposed to identify women leaders who are politically active within the community and not necessarily into the limelight of politics, as well as to look for political talent in unconventional places. She insisted that it was important to ultimately ensure that women run for office and put in place political mentoring programmes, and adequate measures to enable them to raise money to campaign (e.g. 2 million USD are needed to fund a campaign for a 2-year mandate).

Zakia Khattabi, Member of Parliament, Brussels-Capital Region President of the Belgian Green Party at the Senate

Belgian MP Zakia Khattabi provided an insight into the state of play in Belgian politics. According to the Belgian MP, since party members don't know enough about diversity, there is a need to actively integrate the concepts of parity and equality inside parties. She cited some positive and effective measures that her own party applies, such as co-presidency (one woman and one man), gender quotas and the zipper system for the makeup of electoral lists (alternating between one woman and one man candidate). In addition, the Belgian Green Party has a "Green Latino Group." Zakia Khattabi stressed that women are not minorities, and they should not have to justify why they need to be present in politics, because it is their democratic right to expect parity and policies that are developed from a gender perspective and feminist agenda.

The second panel discussed opportunities and challenges accoutered by women who are active in politics at different levels in Europe. Panellists were three mentees from the EWL Political Mentoring Programme, Guliz Tomruk, Sanchia Alasia and Kamilla Sultanova, who answered questions by moderator and MEP Zita Gurmai.

Kamilla Sultanova highlighted the benefits and added-value that minorities bring to Denmark and to the EU, particularly since many Danes from ethnic minorities identify as European, and represent a great potential for Denmark to have a stronger voice in the EU. She deemed it particularly pertinent for women to vote during the upcoming European and national elections in some Member States, if possible with the help of role models to inspire younger women to get involved in politics as voters and candidates alike.

Güliz Tomruk is a candidate to the European elections of May 2014 on the list of the Dutch Green Party. Although this is her first time on a European list, she has been active as a City Councilor in the Netherlands for 10 years. When she was elected in 2004, she was the first woman from an ethnic minority that was selected and elected as City Councilor in her town.

Sanchia Alasia is Councilor for the London Borough of Barking & Dagenham, and an MEP candidate for the Labour Party in London. As an active participant in the EWL political mentoring programme she vouched that "mentoring really works": for example, it provides access to the corridors of power and to networks, and it enables mentors and mentees to learn from each other. Sanchia Alasia called for a wider spread use of political mentoring programmes as a concrete positive measure to address the underrepresentation of women, and more specifically women from ethnic minorities "so that us mentees walking into the European Parliament today will no longer be the exception but a normality."

In Panel 3, partners of the EWL among civil society organisations outlined their recommendations on the political participation of women from diverse backgrounds, and reaffirmed the strong role that civil society needs to play to achieve parity and diversity in political life in Europe.

Moderator and MEP Sirpa Pietikäinen (EPP) opened the floor to Nicoletta Charalambidou, Vice-chair of the European Network against Racism (ENAR), who insisted on the urgent need to mobilise NGOs and their members at national level against increasing xenophobia and populist activities throughout Europe. Referring, in particular, to the EWL video clip on austerity measures which was shown at the beginning of the seminar, she confirmed that austerity measures not only impact more negatively on women, but also contribute to further fueling populist sentiments. ENAR's campaign for the European election, "I vote for Diversity," centers around 7 demands to MEP candidates: to tackle all forms of racism, to develop measures for the inclusion of ethnic minorities, to combat racist violence and hate crime, to measure equality outcomes and impact of EU policies and legislation, to promote equality and diversity in the workplace and in decision-making. In this context, ENAR's Vice-chair insisted on the particular significance of giving migrant women a voice, of securing the right to vote on the basis of residency rather nationality, and of consolidating partnerships with other NGOs, such as with ILGA-Europe on hate crime, and with the European Network of Migrant Women and EWL.

After reaffirming the strategic need for NGO cooperation and active participation during the elections and beyond, Sanja Juras Board Member of ILGA-Europe presented the European LGBTI's movement's "Come Out" campaign for the European elections, including the more detailed 10-point pledge addressed to the candidates for the next European Parliament and the European Commission which ILGA-Europe calls to continue their commitment to human rights generally and LGBTI equality in particular.

The ERGO Network of European Roma Grassroots Organisations was represented by Policy Officer Gabriela Hrabanova who drew the participants' attention on the particular exclusion from political life of Roma women and men in Europe. Although there is a growing yet still limited number of Roma candidates at local elections, there is still a noticeable absence of candidates at national and European elections. Furthermore, Roma candidates' places on lists do not provide them with actual chances of being elected. Particularly in light of Roma people being targeted by populist parties' negative discourse, Gabriela Hrabanova concluded on the urgency for Roma people to vote during the upcoming European and national elections, and for Roma women to participate in politics and decision-making at all levels in Europe.

The seminar was followed by a networking reception.

EWL would like to wholeheartedly thank all moderators, panelists and participants for their interest, commitment and contributions to identify recommendations towards achieving gender equality and diversity in European political life, and a more democratic Europe.

In Rwanda, Widows Take Power After Genocide

Chris McGreal

In previous viewpoints, we've read about the majority women parliament in Rwanda. In the following viewpoint, Chris McGreal interviews a member of that government—a woman who survived the genocide that killed her entire family along with over one million other people. The author interviews others as well, women who survived and came to lead their nation, in the hopes of preventing another genocide. He gives a brief overview of how Rwanda's war led to the majority female government. McGreal is a frequent contributor and former Washington, Johannesburg, and Jerusalem correspondent for the Guardian.

As you read, consider the following questions:

1. What was one of the reasons women widowed in the genocide were forced to fight for their rights, according to the viewpoint?
2. How did property laws in Rwanda change after the genocide?
3. How did the women of Rwanda address the problem of rape laws?

Judith Kanakuze pauses at the mention of her family. "God saved me," she says. "He did not save them." Fourteen years

"We Are the Future," by Chris McGreal, Guardian News and Media Limited, December 17, 2008. Reprinted by permission.

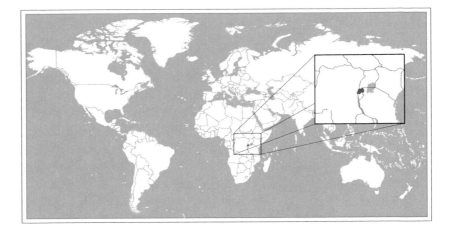

ago, 11,000 Tutsis were murdered in Kanakuze's home province of Kibuye, in the west of Rwanda, in the town's Roman Catholic church. Almost everyone in her extended family had fled to the chapel for sanctuary. The next day another 10,000 people were murdered in the town stadium in a pogrom led by Kibuye's governor.

Kanakuze does not want to say much more. The survivors of the genocide often speak of the pain of being "condemned to live." But she admits to an unexpected optimism as a member of the first parliament in the world to have a majority of female MPs. "This is a different time," she says. "We are transforming our society, and women are part of the solution."

In September, Rwanda's parliamentary election saw women win 45 of the 80 seats. Nearly half were elected in women-only seats, with the rest triumphing in open ballots.

The women MPs include former rebels and genocide survivors, war widows and peasant farmers, and although the election was a landmark, the women's success was not unexpected. Under the requirements of a new constitution, women already held a third of cabinet posts—including the foreign, education and information portfolios. The heads of the supreme court and the police are also women, as are a majority of the country's prison governors.

Before 1994, women held only around one in five parliamentary seats. The genocide changed everything. When the killing ended there were twice as many women as men in Rwanda, and while the gap has since narrowed, more than a third of households are still headed by women. Women also make up 55% of the workforce and own about 40% of businesses.

Aloisea Inyumba is a Tutsi former rebel fighter, who has been part of the Rwandan Patriotic Front-led (RPF) government since it overthrew the extremist Hutu regime in 1994—serving first as minister for women and the family, before moving to the gender and social affairs brief. She is now a senator in the upper house of parliament, and says that women began to exert political muscle partly as a means of survival. When the killing ended, widows were sometimes left destitute because the existing law didn't permit women to inherit land or property.

That prompted Inyumba to press for change. "After the genocide there were property disputes," she says, "so we worked on a strong family bill. For the first time the women of this country were given rights to inherit. Traditionally, if a woman married a man, the property belonged to him. If your husband died, the property would go to the in-laws. This bill has become a legal protection for families. Women can now inherit, women can own property. A girl child and a boy child have equal entitlement to inheritance."

Another issue that women forced the government to address is rape. Sexual attacks were an integral part of the genocide, with local political leaders running what amounted to rape camps in some villages.

The international tribunal for Rwanda—which tried some of the organisers and perpetrators of the killings—defined rape as an act of genocide under international law, if part of a systematic move to wipe out an ethnic group. Yet when it came to Rwanda's own law to punish genocide, rape was almost relegated to a relatively minor offence. The draft genocide law split offences into four categories, with sentences of death or life imprisonment for murder. But rape was placed in the lowest category, alongside offences such as looting, with the draft law requiring only a light prison sentence or community service.

Groups such as the Widows of the Genocide and Ibuka, the survivors' association, were outraged. Many Tutsi women who had been raped had been infected with HIV, while others bore the children of their attackers. "The women were not happy with that draft law," says Inyumba, and so "we advocated for a change. We regarded the genocide law as very important in ensuring that the issue of sexual abuse was taken seriously. There was a proposal and an agreement that all the issues dealing with sexual violence would be included as category one. That was a great victory for women."

As the politicians moved beyond the immediate legacy of genocide, Kanakuze joined the committee that was drafting a constitution, as a "gender expert." She pressed for the 2003 constitution to require that at least 30% of seats in parliament and the cabinet be held by women. "Before we were listened to on social issues and gender equality and about violence against women," she says. "But now women will be a majority on the committees that were controlled by men—security, finance."

This transformation seems all the more unlikely given that it was engineered by what had been a male-dominated rebel group. But Inyumba says a focus on gender equality infused the RPF from the start because the party was focused on a broader rejection of discrimination of all kinds—beginning with the official persecution of Tutsis by successive Rwandan Hutu administrations. "The important generation is the next generation," she says hopefully. "My children are 20 and 18. They do not speak this language of ethnicity."

But many Rwandans still do and the government's critics say that discrimination is being only papered over. Public recognition of ethnicity is officially discouraged but that cannot hide the fact that a new Tutsi political elite—mostly made up of former exiles— has emerged dominant and privileged. Only 15% of the Rwandan population are Tutsi, and it has not gone unnoticed that a sizeable number of the new women MPs are of this ethnicity, leading some to question how well they can represent the mass of Hutu women who live in poverty.

MP Euthalie Nyirabega declines to discuss her ethnicity, but says that although she went on to become a sociology professor at the national university, her background is close to the grass roots poor. She served in local government and in a number of women's organisations before being elected to parliament. "I'm from a rural area," she says. "It's important that people in this building understand what women in rural areas are thinking. Not everyone here has that background."

Men have, on the whole, remained silent on the new laws. But Evarist Kalish MP, a member of the Liberal party and the chair of parliament's human rights committee, says that many men recognise that women may provide the best leadership.

"More than men, women are the victims of the war," says Kalish. "They have different priorities to those of men. They have more concern about issues related to violence in general, and gender-based violence in particular. Women have faced discrimination so they want to put a stop to discrimination. All of this will contribute to preventing another genocide."

Periodical and Internet Sources Bibliography

The following articles have been selected to supplement the diverse views presented in this chapter.

Sahsa Arutyunova, Earl Wilson, and Chris Delmas, "Democrats, Looking Ahead to 2020, See a Future That Is Female," *New York Times*, October 19, 2018. https://www.nytimes.com/2018/10/19 /us/politics/on-politics-democratic-women-2020.html.

Lily Hindy, "Kuwaiti Women Leaders Aim to Bring More Gender Parity to Politics," Century Foundation, June 13, 2018. https://tcf .org/content/report/kuwaiti-women-leaders-aim-bring-gender -parity-politics/?session=1.

Sallyann Nicholls, "Women in Politics: How Does Europe Measure Up?," Euronews, updated December 3, 2018. https://www .euronews.com/2018/03/12/women-in-politics-how-does -europe-measure-up-.

Motoko Rich, "Japan Ranks Low in Female Lawmakers. An Election Won't Change That," *New York Times*, October 21, 2017. https:// www.nytimes.com/2017/10/21/world/asia/japan-women -election-politics.html.

Nurfilzah Rohaidi, "The Key to Asia's Success? More Women at the Top," GovInsider, October 3, 2018. https://govinsider.asia /inclusive-gov/the-key-to-asias-success-more-women-at-the-top.

Damien Sharkov, "Russians Grow Cold on Women in Politics as Majority Oppose Female President," *Newsweek*, March 3, 2017. https://www.newsweek.com/russians-grow-cold-women-politics -majority-oppose-female-president-563363.

Kallie Szczepanski, "Female Heads of State in Asia," ThoughtCo., updated July 16, 2018. https://www.thoughtco.com/female-heads -of-state-in-asia-195688.

Alison Trowsdale, "The Power-Sharing Dream: Where Women Rule in the World," BBC News, July 15, 2018. https://www.bbc.com /news/world-44454914.

For Further Discussion

Chapter 1

1. The viewpoints in this chapter illustrate that gender diversity in governments varies considerably from country to country, with some of the most diverse not being the ones you might expect. After reading this chapter, how do you account for these surprises?
2. The last viewpoint suggests that LGBT candidates are making swift progress—much faster than women have in the past. What cultural or political factors account for that? Do you think the trend will continue?

Chapter 2

1. In the third viewpoint in this chapter, Laura Liswood suggests that a woman must be likable in order to be elected US president, but that is not necessarily the case for a man. After reading the other viewpoints in this volume, do you have any ideas why this might be the case? Do you think a woman who was more likable than Hillary Clinton could have won the 2016 election? Would a male candidate who was more likable than Donald Trump have won by a greater margin and taken the popular vote as well as the electoral college?
2. In the last viewpoint in this chapter, Mark R. Thompson explains how stereotypes about women can actually make it easier for them to be elected in troubled times. Can you think of examples of how that might work in Western democracies? Might something similar have been going on in the 2018 US midterm elections when a record number of women were elected to both state and national offices?

Chapter 3

1. The viewpoints in this chapter suggest that despite the many women leaders who have been elected around the world, sexism is still a huge problem for women politicians. Can you think of any recent examples of this? Can you think of a female world leader who doesn't seem to have a problem with sexism?
2. In viewpoint 6 in this chapter, the author discusses the murder of British MP Jo Cox. How do you think the political climate contributed to her death? Do any others, besides the man who shot and stabbed her, bear responsibility for her death? Why or why not?

Chapter 4

1. The viewpoints in this chapter have looked at ways to increase gender diversity in the world's governments. After reading them, do you feel that the future will be more equal?
2. After reading the viewpoints in this chapter, do you think that having more women in positions of power, whether by quotas or other means, will result in better opportunities and greater equality for all women?

Organizations to Contact

The editors have compiled the following list of organizations concerned with the issues debated in this book. The descriptions are derived from materials provided by the organizations. All have publications or information available for interested readers. The list was compiled on the date of publication of the present volume; the information provided here may change. Be aware that many organizations take several weeks or longer to respond to inquiries, so allow as much time as possible.

Canadian Women's Foundation (CWF)
133 Richmond Street W., Suite 504
Toronto, ON, Canada M5H 2L3
phone: (416) 365-1444
website: https://www.canadianwomen.org

The CWF is a public foundation that focuses on helping women and girls improve gender equality and economic conditions for everyone. It works with community organizations to address four primary issues: prevention of gender-based violence, women's economic development, girls' empowerment, and inclusive leadership. The CWF's definition of women includes people who identify as women, girls, trans, genderqueer, and gender non-binary.

Center for American Women in Politics (CAWP)
191 Ryders Lane
New Brunswick, NJ 08901
phone: (848) 932-9384
email: cawp.info@eagleton.rutgers.edu
website: http://www.cawp.rutgers.edu

A part of the Eagleton Institute of Politics, the CAWP is dedicated to promoting greater knowledge and understanding about women's participation in politics and government and to enhancing women's influence and leadership in public life.

Equal Voice
116 Albert, Suite 810
Ottawa, ON, Canada K1P 5G3
phone: (613) 236-0302
email: Info@equalvoice.ca
website: https://www.equalvoice.ca/index.cfm

Equal Voice is a national, bilingual, multipartisan organization dedicated to electing women to all levels of political office in Canada.

Girls in Politics
1200 G Street NW
Washington, DC 20005
phone: (202) 660-1457, ext. 2
email: Info@girlsinpolitics.org
website: http://www.girlsinpolitics.org

Girls in Politics is an initiative of the Political Institute for Women. It introduces girls ages eight to seventeen to politics, policy, the work of the US Congress, parliamentary governments, and the United Nations.

International Women's Democracy Center (IWDC)
1726 M Street NW, Suite 1100
Washington, DC 20036
phone: (202) 530-0563
email: Info@iwdc.org
website: https://iwdc.org

The IWDC partners with established nongovernmental organizations and local leaders around the world. It provides training for women in order to increase their political participation at the local, state, and national levels. The IWDC also conducts research on how to increase the participation of women in politics, policy, and decision making in their own countries.

National Council of Women of Canada
Le Conseil National des Femmes du Canada
PO Box 67099
Ottawa, ON, Canada K2A 4E4
phone: (902) 422-8485
email: Pres@ncwcanda.com
website: http://www.ncwcanada.com

The National Council of Women of Canada is an organization of women working to bring to the attention of government various issues of that affect families and communities.

National Organization for Women
1100 H Street NW, Suite 300
Washington, DC 20005
phone: (202) 628-8669
website: https://now.org

Founded in 1966, the National Organization for Women is a grassroots arm of the women's movement. It is dedicated to many issues and many approaches to fighting for women's rights. It has hundreds of chapters, some in all fifty states, and hundreds of thousands of members, many of whom are dedicated activists for the cause of women's rights.

Running Start
1310 L Street NW
Washington, DC 20005
phone: (202) 223-3895
email: Info@runningstartonline.org
website: http://runningstartonline.org

Running Start is a nonprofit organization that educates young women about politics and trains them in the skills they need to be leaders.

Teach a Girl to Lead (TAG)
191 Ryders Lane
New Brunswick, NJ 08901
phone: (732) 932-6778
email: Tag@eagleton.rutgers.edu
website: http://tag.rutgers.edu

A project of the Center for American Women in Politics, TAG helps young people rethink leadership so they can imagine women in leaderships roles.

UN Women
220 E. Forty-Second Street
New York, NY 10017
phone: (646) 781-4400
website: www.unwomen.org

UN Women, a part of the United Nations, is a worldwide organization dedicated to the empowerment of women. The organization works with member states to set standards for reaching gender equality and meeting the needs of women and girls throughout the world.

Women's International League for Peace and Freedom/Peace Women Project (WILPF)
777 United Nations Plaza, 6th Floor
New York, NY 10017
phone: (202) 682-1265
email: Info@peacewomen.org
website: http://peacewomen.org

The priority of the WILPF is to address the root causes of violence with a feminist lens and nonviolent action. The Peace Women Project of the organization promotes the role of women in preventing conflict by strengthening women's meaningful participation and promoting the equal and full participation of women in all efforts to create and maintain international peace and security.

Women's Learning Partnership (WLP)
4343 Montgomery Avenue, Suite 201
Bethesda, MD 20814
phone: (301) 654-2774
email: wlp@learningpartnership.org
website: https://learningpartnership.org
The WLP is a partnership of twenty individual women's rights organizations that promote women's leadership, civic engagement, and civil rights. The WLP works particularly in Muslim-majority societies to empower women to transform their families, communities, and societies.

Bibliography of Books

Mary Beard, *Women in Power: A Manifesto*. New York, NY: Liveright, 2017.

Helene Cooper, "*Madame President: The Extraordinary Journey of Ellen Johnson Sirleaf*. New York, NY: Simon and Schuster, 2017.

Jane Sherron De Hart, *Ruth Bader Ginsburg: A Life*. New York, NY: Knopf, 2018.

Lillian Faderman, *Harvey Milk: His Lives and Death*. New Haven, CT: Yale University Press, 2018.

Nikki Haley, *Can't Is Not an Option: My American Story*. New York, NY: Sentinel, 2012.

Jay Newton-Small, *Broad Influence: How Women Are Changing the Way America Works*. New York, NY: Time Books, 2016.

Susan Madsen, ed., *Women and Leadership Around the World*. Charlotte, NC: Information Age Publishing, 2015.

Ellen R. Malcolm, *When Women Win: Emily's List and the Rise of Women in American Politics*. Boston, MA: Houghton Mifflin Harcourt, 2016.

Sally G. McMillen, *Seneca Falls and the Origins of the Women's Rights Movement*. Oxford, UK: Oxford University Press, 2008.

Joyce Marie Mushaben, *Becoming Madam Chancellor: Angela Merkel and the Berlin Republic*. Cambridge, UK: Cambridge University Press, 2017.

Alyse Nelson, *Vital Voices: The Power of Women Leading Change Around the World*. New York, NY: Jossey-Bass, 2012.

Jennifer Palmieri, *Dear Madam President: An Open Letter to the Women Who Will Run the World*. New York, NY: Grand Central, 2018.

Rena Pederson, *The Burma Spring: Aung San Suu Kyi and the New Struggle for the Soul of a Nation.* New York, NY: Pegasus, 2015.

Andrew Reynolds, *The Children of Harvey Milk: How LGBTQ Politicians Changed the World.* Oxford, UK: Oxford University Press, 2019.

Condoleeza Rice, *No Higher Honor: A Memoir of My Years in Washington.* New York, NY: Broadway Books, 2011.

Valerie Sperling, *Sex, Politics, and Putin: Political Legitimacy in Russia.* Oxford, UK: Oxford University Press, 2015.

Susan Thomson, *Rwanda: From Genocide to Precarious Peace.* New Haven, CT: Yale University Press, 2018.

Richard L. Zweigenhaft and G. William Domhoff, *Diversity in the Power Elite: Ironies and Unfulfilled Promises.* 3rd ed. Lanham, MD: Rowman and Littlefield, 2018.

Index

V

W